The Farm Kitchen

Dedicated to all my grandchildren

The Farm Kitchen

PHOTOGRAPHY & TEXT BY RUSSEL WASSERFALL

RECIPES COMPILED BY COLETTE, CAMILLA & JASON COMINS

Acknowledgements

The first installment of the Country Kitchen appeared in *SA Country Life* magazine in March 2004. It was to run as a monthly feature on self-sufficiency, mixed farming and recipes for the next fifteen months and it was the beginning of the journey that led to us creating this book. Editor Margaret Wasserfall has been an inspiration and become a respected friend and I am grateful for her encouragement.

My mother, Julia Havemann, taught me strength and a love of food and gardening that have combined to make me the curious cook and kitchen gardener I am today. That curiosity has led me to always seek out new ingredients to grow in my vegetable patch and to find inspiration from fellow cooks and chefs in the books and magazines that I consume voraciously.

It is impossible to name all those who have enriched our lives on the farm. This includes all the friends and family, international clients and cooking school students who have appreciated our food.

But the most important contributors to this book are my family. My husband Trevor has worked tirelessly to provide this life we all enjoy and he and my oldest son Clayton are never shy of praise for the food that is the fruit of their efforts as well as my own. There is absolutely nothing more precious to me than sitting in the warmth of my kitchen with them and with my daughter Camilla and youngest son Jason, lingering over empty plates and debating about what we will cook for the next meal.

COLETTE COMINS

First published in 2006 by Struik Publishers (a division of New Holland Publishing (South Africa) (Pty) Ltd)
www.struik.co.za

Cornelis Struik House, 80 McKenzie Street, Cape Town 8001, South Africa
Garfield House, 86–88 Edgware Road, London W2 2EA, United Kingdom
14 Aquatic Drive, Frenchs Forest, NSW 2086, Australia
218 Lake Road, Northcote, Auckland, New Zealand

New Holland Publishing is a member of Johnnic Communications Ltd

10 9 8 7 6 5 4 3 2 1

PUBLISHING MANAGER: Linda de Villiers
EDITOR: Joy Clack
DESIGNER: Beverley Dodd
PHOTOGRAPHER: Russel Wasserfall
PROOFREADER: Tessa Kennedy

Reproduction by Hirt & Carter Cape (Pty) Ltd
Printed and bound by Kyodo Printing Co (Singapore) Pte Ltd

ISBN 1 77007 262 4
ISBN 9 781770 072626

Contents

Introduction

By Russel Wasserfall

This is a book about food and recipes, but it is also a book about a family of cooks right on the cutting edge of a world movement. There is a massive trend worldwide to downscale, to move back to the country from big, frenetic cities, and to live a simpler, slower life. Hand in hand with this tendency is the change in our eating habits and fashions.

Slow food has taken off, and people are visiting organic and farmers' markets looking for real food to cook for their families. They are looking for recipes that make the most of the best ingredients. There has been a resurgence in regional cuisines; instead of merely Italian food, diners seek out Ligurian, Tuscan or Calabrian specialities. Grandma's recipe book is suddenly very much in vogue.

On their farm outside Vryheid in northern KwaZulu-Natal, Trevor and Colette Comins are not particularly concerned with world trends. They are more focused on what's for dinner. Depending on who's around the breakfast table on any given morning, influences on the menu will vary, but the conversation never does. It's always about food.

It might be just the family around the kitchen table, but there may also be a few friends staying in the guest cottages. If there are students in for a cooking course, lunch and dinner will be products of the day's lessons. Meals for birders on a crane safari will include the best produce the farm has to offer, while in winter, American bird hunters will be treated to game, wild fowl and fish dishes from the area's lands, rivers and dams.

At 142 hectares, the farm itself is not very big, but its impression is much larger than the sum of its parts. Trevor and his oldest son, Clayton, run a small herd of Nguni cattle. Trevor was raised at Tugela Ferry and is profoundly and proudly influenced by Zulu culture and language, in which he is completely fluent. The traditional cattle are herded with deference to their cultural importance and are raised on the veld and on organic winter feed. An ox or two are always on hand, being fattened for the kitchen.

Mixed farming is the name of the game here though. There are crops of maize and sorghum, pumpkins and winter feed like oats and Japanese radish for the cattle. The vegetable patches and fruit trees take up about an acre all told and this provides more than enough for the family, the school and endless rounds of preserves and pickles.

Any excess, as well as organic offcuts from kitchen preparation, goes to the pigs. As a result, they produce the sweetest organically raised pork you are ever likely to eat. The farm teeters right on the edge of being self-sufficient. Eggs, chickens, milk, beef, cheese, pork, fruit, vegetables and herbs – it's like having a big organic market outside the kitchen door. Then of course there's the hunting and foraging, which produces game and fish, mushrooms and berries and plenty of stories to keep guests entertained.

The day begins early on Sterkstroom farm, and you are as likely to be woken by the rooster as you are by Colette, in the vegetable garden, yelling about the 'damn duiker' eating her beans again. There are constant visits to the garden during the day, but the morning inspection is vital. If you know what's ripe or ready in either of the two main patches, you might have an advantage in the debate about what to cook that day.

8

If there's a theme to the food in this book, then it's fresh ingredients and quality produce prepared with love. It's not French or Italian food, but a mixture of everything. There are elements of classic cooking with stocks and sauces and popular European dishes, but it is not hidebound. Influences range as far as Chinese and Spanish. It's about what's fresh in the garden and what it can be turned into.

No one on the farm follows any particular discipline. Camilla, the oldest of Colette and Trevor's children, once worked for six weeks in San Francisco's Chinatown with a well-known chef to learn about real Chinese food. She did a pasta course at the Cipriani Hotel in Venice with Marcella Hazzan because she wanted to cook pasta better. She originally trained at the Christina Martin School in Durban and then with the Mövenpick hotel group in Germany, and has built extensively on that base, working as a food stylist, restaurant consultant and commercial recipe developer.

Jason, Camilla's youngest brother, trained in Ireland at the Ballymaloe School under Darina Allen. His speciality is cooking fish and he likes the science of making processed meat products. Always looking for new recipes and techniques, he befriended a German monk from the local monastery in Vryheid and learned the recipes for a number of Bavarian cold meats and sausages. When he's not fishing, hunting or teaching cooking, he's in the kitchen or smokehouse, fiddling around with bacon or some other delicacy.

Both Camilla and Jason are powerfully influenced by their mother's unquenchable desire to constantly learn more and do more with everyday ingredients. When Colette and Trevor were first married, he was a game ranger living and working at a remote post on Itala Game Reserve. Even then, her love of food was not dampened by the fact that the absence of electricity and amenities forced her to beat the egg white topping for perfect lemon meringue pie with a table fork.

That love of food and the incredible work ethic remains with her today, along with an insatiable curiosity. If Colette has a spare moment, she's off on a cheese-making course, building henhouses for free range chickens or reading about how to enrich their chickens' eggs by feeding them marigolds. If Colette tastes a rhubarb pie she likes, she won't only go home and try to reproduce it in her kitchen, she'll grow the rhubarb for it and encourage her chickens to lay tastier eggs to improve the pastry.

It is her curiosity that drives the constant evolution of the food. Bread is a prime example of this. Students at the cooking school, whether they do a fun weekend course or a week- or month-long syllabus, bake a different bread every day. The recipes have been gleaned and developed from numerous sources. For instance, fishing trips to Mozambique brought Colette into contact with Portuguese bread made with a potato starter. Determined to make it herself, she came home, found a potato starter recipe and started experimenting with the bread until she had it right. In fact, she took it even further. After seeing this bread being baked in a wood-fired oven on Inhaca Island, and loving the flavour the fire imparted, she became determined to have one of her own. This led to months of intensive research and planning before a local builder was roped in to assemble it. The oven stands on a purpose-built patio outside the cooking school and is used not only for bread, but also for pizza, roasts and baked dishes of all kinds.

A few years ago, around the beginning of 2002, *Country Life* magazine started getting faxes from The Farm Cooking School. When response to the faxes was slow, the phone calls started. Trevor was convinced that his family farm and their various doings would make a great feature for the magazine. It turns out he was right, and my visit to Sterkstroom farm in northern KwaZulu-Natal proved to be the first of many.

I wrote and photographed a series of articles for *Country Life* that ran for nearly two years. In them, we brought the story of the Comins family and their little farm to readers in South Africa and abroad. When the series ended, there were calls for more, and particularly for more recipes, and so the idea for this book was born.

Because food is their life, you cannot separate the recipes the Comins cooks have created in these pages from the lives they lead. When you first pick it up, this will appear to be a recipe book, but it is really about country life, about self-sufficiency, about living close to nature and eating her bounty fresh from the earth. It is also the story of an exceptional family who calmly get on with a life that is increasingly seen, on an international stage, as the most desirable lifestyle. What a joy to grow your own vegetables, raise a few cows or chickens, and cook something whose provenance you are absolutely sure of. Aren't days sweeter that are defined by the rising and setting of the sun and not how busy the gym is going to be if you don't get there by 7 am?

There is no diet food in the pages that follow; Colette just wouldn't have it. However, there is a lot to be said for changing your diet and eating something that has been grown with love. What's to stop you building a brick oven in your back yard and baking your own bread? Farmers' markets have really started to come into their own in major centres. By supporting them, you support small producers and a whole network of people who are trying to bring healthier produce to consumers.

A revolution is happening around the world, where people are ignoring packet sauces and going back to cooking wholesome meals from scratch using the best ingredients they can find. The Comins family never intended to be part of this movement, or any other movement for that matter, it just happened. Colette collected and devised new recipes and kept expanding her vegetable garden and the orchard.

Her philosophy of fresh ingredients used in the right season and of producing as much as possible on the farm seemed natural to her. As for organic production methods, that's just common sense. Why would she spray poison on something she intends her family to eat in the very near future? They need to be healthy so they can congregate around the breakfast table each morning and debate the day's menu: How to get the best out of the carrots; which variety of potato would make better mash; what to do with all those raspberries that are ripening beneath the fig tree. No thoughts of being at the centre of a culinary revolution; all they have ever wanted is to eat well and share their bounty with anyone who stops by for a visit.

In this book, we are not intending to inspire everyone to drop everything and move to the country. We just set out to provide a glimpse into the Comins' farm kitchen and a slower life. These dishes are designed to feed families, big or small. They glorify the flavour of individual ingredients or celebrate the bounty of a bumper harvest. Hopefully some of the recipes will rekindle your love of eating, help you to experience the joy of cooking with fresh, seasonal produce and just slow down.

You don't have to move to a farm to do it. If you take a window box and grow some tomatoes it will be a great step. Heading for a farmers' market to get some vegetables for the week would help change your pace a bit. Even if one day you just eat a raspberry hot from the sun and fresh from the plant, Colette will be tickled pink.

Light Salads
& Appetizers

It can get unbelievably hot on the farm during summer. No matter how hard you work during the course of a long summer day, the prospect of a big farm meal at lunch or dinner is not exactly inviting in such hot weather. We tend to be light but frequent eaters in summer, leaning heavily on the vegetable garden for inspiration and fresh, light produce. Here are some of our favourite snacky meals – we particularly enjoy doing a sort of Mediterranean mezze thing with a couple of salads, perhaps a quiche and some Baba Ghanoush (page 30) and flat bread. Lots of flavours and cool dressings make the meal interesting and you can choose exactly how much you want to eat by taking little bits of whatever you fancy.

Simple Salad

This recipe requires the freshest ingredients, preferably straight from the garden. We serve it with our crusty Portuguese Potato Bread (page 138) to mop up the dressing.

3 heads cos or butter lettuce
1 large bunch radish
Maldon® sea salt and freshly ground black pepper

DRESSING
50 ml red wine vinegar
100 ml extra virgin olive oil
1 large clove garlic, crushed
5 ml Dijon mustard
5 ml sugar
5 ml salt

Make the dressing first by whisking together all the ingredients in a jug. Set aside to infuse.

Wash and drip-dry the lettuce and place in a large salad bowl. Thinly slice the radish onto the lettuce and drizzle with the dressing. Season with salt and pepper, toss and serve immediately.

SERVES 6

Beetroot Salad

10 medium beetroot

2 onions

borage flowers to garnish

DRESSING

100 ml balsamic vinegar

50 ml extra virgin olive oil

5 ml sugar

15 ml chopped fresh tarragon

salt and freshly ground black pepper

Boil and peel the beetroot and allow to cool – you can do this the day before if you like. Finely slice the onions and soak them in cold water for 30 minutes to sweeten. Slice the beetroot into rounds, place in a salad bowl and top with the drained onion rings.

To make the dressing, mix together the balsamic vinegar, olive oil, sugar, tarragon and salt and pepper and pour over the beetroot and onions. Toss to mix, then garnish with the borage flowers and serve.

SERVES 6

Indian Tomato Soup

30 ml sunflower oil

1 large onion, finely chopped

3 bay leaves

1 stick cinnamon

12 peppercorns

15 ml ground cumin

15 ml garam masala

3 x 410 g tins chopped tomatoes

10 ml sugar

500 ml chicken or vegetable stock

pinch of salt

1 small bunch fresh coriander

naan breads for serving

Heat the oil in a medium, heavy-based saucepan. Fry the onion, bay leaves, cinnamon and peppercorns and cook until the onion is soft. Add the cumin, garam masala, tomatoes, sugar and stock and bring to the boil slowly. Reduce the heat and allow the soup to simmer for 30 minutes. Strain through a metal sieve, using the back of a spoon to extract as much liquid as possible. Reheat the soup and season with salt. Garnish with coriander and serve with naan bread.

SERVES 4–6

Avocado Salad with Dill & Yoghurt Dressing

3 heads butter lettuce

3 perfectly ripe avocados

200 g calamata olives

DRESSING

30 ml plain yoghurt

30 ml chopped fresh dill

50 ml white wine vinegar

100 ml extra virgin olive oil

2 cloves garlic, peeled and crushed

5 ml sugar

5 ml salt

Make the dressing first by whisking together all the ingredients. Set aside.

Wash and drip-dry the lettuce, then break it into bite-sized pieces and scatter over an attractive serving platter. Slice the avocados and arrange on top of the lettuce, followed by the olives. Drizzle with the dressing. We usually serve this salad with our Russian Haddock Pie (page 126).

SERVES 6

Green Bean Salad

10 baby potatoes, boiled in their jackets and halved

250 g blanched green beans

4 hard-boiled eggs, chopped

60 ml snipped chives

extra chives to garnish

DRESSING

100 ml raspberry vinegar (substitute red wine vinegar if you can't get your
    hands on the raspberry version)

200 ml olive oil

1 clove garlic, peeled and crushed

5 ml Dijon mustard

salt and freshly ground black pepper

Make the dressing first by mixing the raspberry vinegar, olive oil, garlic, mustard, salt and pepper together. Set aside.

Place the still-warm, halved baby potatoes on a platter and dress with half the salad dressing. Add the green beans, chopped egg, chives and the remainder of the dressing. Garnish with the extra chives and serve at once otherwise the beans will oxidize and discolour.

SERVES 4–6

Roasted Peppers

6–8 red, green and/or yellow peppers
30 ml olive oil
15 ml balsamic vinegar
salt and freshly ground black pepper
rocket leaves
Parmesan cheese shavings

Preheat the oven to 230 °C (450 °F, Gas Mark 8). Brush each pepper thoroughly with olive oil, place on a baking sheet and roast in the oven for 15–20 minutes. Turn regularly until the skin bubbles and blackens all over. Remove from the oven, cover with clingfilm or a plastic shopping bag so that the peppers sweat. Set aside to cool completely. Peel off the skin and remove the seeds. Slice the flesh into long strips and dress with balsamic vinegar and salt and pepper to taste. Serve with rocket and Parmesan shavings.

SERVES 4

24

Roasted Pepper Tart

23 cm tin lined with shortcrust pastry and baked blind (see Basics, page 216)
3 red peppers
200 ml fresh cream
3 eggs
salt and freshly ground black pepper
6 fresh basil leaves

Preheat the oven to 180 °C (350 °F, Gas Mark 4). Roast the peppers as described on page 24 and slice into thin strips. Whisk together the cream and eggs and season with salt and pepper. Arrange the peppers and torn basil leaves on the base of the baked pastry shell. Pour the cream mixture over the peppers and bake for 20–25 minutes until the custard has just set. Serve warm with the Simple Salad (page 18).

SERVES 4–6

Grilled Red Peppers

The difference between roasted and grilled peppers is that roasted peppers are done in an oven and grilled peppers are done on the open fire. The latter has a slightly smoky flavour.

6 large red peppers
50 ml olive oil
25 ml red wine vinegar
2 cloves garlic, peeled and crushed
pinch of sugar
salt and freshly ground black pepper
rocket leaves for serving

Over a large gas stovetop place three peppers at a time to grill. If you don't have a gas stove, you can do this directly on hot coals in a barbecue (braai) – in fact, this adds a wonderful, smoky flavour. Turn the peppers as each side is chargrilled. When the peppers are grilled, place in a bowl and cover with clingfilm to sweat until completely cool. Place under cold running water to help remove the skin. Slice thinly, discard the seeds and mix together with the olive oil, vinegar, garlic and sugar. Season to taste and serve with fresh rocket.

SERVES 6–8

Baked Chicken Liver Pâté

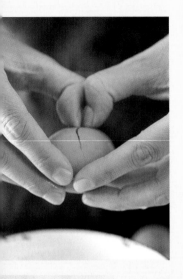

6 spring onions, chopped

50 g butter

250 g chicken livers

250 ml fresh cream

3 eggs

2.5 ml grated nutmeg

2.5 ml ground cloves

salt and freshly ground black pepper

100 ml port or sherry

100 ml melted, clarified butter

Preheat the oven to 160 °C (325 °F, Gas Mark 3). Gently sauté the spring onions in the butter. Set aside to cool. Rinse the chicken livers and place in a blender with the cream and eggs. Blend until smooth. Add the seasonings, spring onions and port and blend again. Strain through a sieve and pour into four 10 cm-diameter ramekins. Place in a *bain-marie* and bake for 25–30 minutes until firm to the touch. Allow to cool before pouring the clarified butter over the top. Serve with hot crusty bread topped with Red Wine Onion Marmalade (page 213).

MAKES 4 LARGE RAMEKINS

Baba Ghanoush

We usually roast the aubergines in the outdoor oven while the fire is still heating it for baking bread. This gives the baba ghanoush a wonderful, smoky flavour.

4 aubergines (brinjals)
olive oil for roasting
salt and freshly ground black pepper
3 cloves garlic, peeled
juice of 1 large lemon
2.5 ml paprika
50 ml chopped fresh parsley
100 ml olive oil

Preheat the oven to 240 °C (475 °F, Gas Mark 9). Place the aubergines in a roasting pan, brush with olive oil and season with salt and pepper. Roast for about 45 minutes until soft. Remove from the oven and allow to cool. Peel off the skin and place the pulp, garlic, lemon juice, paprika, parsley and olive oil in a blender. Blend until smooth. Season with salt and pepper, spoon into a serving dish and garnish with an extra sprinkling of paprika. Serve with Portuguese rolls or focaccia as part of a mezze platter.

SERVES 8–10

Asian Tomato Salsa

We love to eat this with Baba Ghanoush (page 30), Roasted Peppers (page 24) and Focaccia (page 146).

8 ripe plum tomatoes
1 red onion, finely chopped
1 green chilli, seeded and finely chopped
15 ml sesame seed oil
30 ml rice wine vinegar
5 ml sugar
30 ml chopped fresh coriander
salt and freshly ground black pepper

Seed the tomatoes and chop finely. Mix in all the remaining ingredients and allow to infuse for about 15 minutes before serving with your choice of bread.

SERVES 4–6

Tabbouleh

250 g bulgur (burghul) wheat

8 plum tomatoes

1 cucumber

6 spring onions

1 bunch fresh mint

1 bunch fresh Italian parsley

juice and zest of 2 lemons

salt and freshly ground black pepper

pinch of sugar

100 ml olive oil

4 heads cos lettuce

Prepare the bulgur wheat according to the instructions on the packet. Chop the tomatoes, cucumber and spring onions and add to the prepared, cooled wheat. Chop the mint and parsley and add to the mixture along with the lemon zest. Mix together and season with salt, pepper and sugar.

Just before serving mix together the lemon juice and olive oil and dress the salad. Transfer to the centre of a platter and arrange the cos lettuce leaves around. The lettuce leaves are used like spoons to eat the salad.

SERVES 8

Buckwheat Blinis with Smoked Salmon

225 g buckwheat flour

2.5 ml salt

1 x 10 g packet instant yeast

5 ml sugar

375 ml lukewarm water

225 g cake (plain) flour

375 ml lukewarm milk

2 whole eggs

1 egg, separated

oil for frying

375 ml horseradish cream

800 g smoked salmon slices

caviar (optional) and fresh dill to garnish

In large bowl, mix the buckwheat flour, salt, instant yeast and sugar. Add the water and stir until it forms a smooth paste. Cover with clingfilm and leave to rise for 15 minutes. In another bowl, place the cake flour, milk, whole eggs and egg yolk and whisk together until smooth. Stir the buckwheat mixture into the cake flour mixture and blend by hand until smooth. Cover and set aside to rise for 2 hours until double in volume. Whisk the egg white until stiff peaks form, then fold into the risen mixture before frying. Heat a heavy-based frying pan and add a little oil. Place tablespoonfuls of the mixture into the pan and cook until the bubbles begin to rise, then turn each blini over and cook the other side. Do this in batches and set aside until ready to serve.

Sandwich two blinis with a dollop of horseradish cream and top with a generous helping of smoked salmon and a sprinkling of ground black pepper. Garnish with a dollop of caviar (if using) and a sprig of dill.

SERVES 8

34

Green Tomato Tarte Tatin

20 ml butter

10 ml olive oil

20 ml sugar

8 green tomatoes, halved

400 g ready-to-roll puff pastry

1 red onion, finely sliced

30 g Parmesan cheese shavings

15–20 rocket leaves

15 ml balsamic vinegar

salt and freshly ground black pepper

Preheat the oven to 240 °C (475 °F, Gas Mark 9). Melt the butter in an ovenproof 25 cm pan over medium heat. Add the olive oil and sugar and caramelize until lightly golden. Arrange the tomatoes, cut side down and as tightly as possible, in the pan. Reduce the heat to low and cook for 3–4 minutes, then remove from the heat.

Roll out the pastry on a lightly floured surface and cut out a 30 cm diameter circle. Place the pastry circle over the tomatoes, pushing down lightly. Place the pan in the oven and bake for 30–35 minutes until the pastry is golden brown and cooked. Allow to cool for 10 minutes before inverting the tart onto a serving platter. If the tart looks a little underdone when inverted, then place under the grill for 5 minutes. Garnish with the red onion, Parmesan and rocket. Drizzle with balsamic vinegar and season with salt and pepper before serving.

SERVES 6

Courgette Blossom & Green Tomato Tempura

Tempura is a method of Japanese-style deep-frying. The way to master it is to make sure that the oil is hot and deep, the ingredient used for dipping into the batter is dry, the liquid used to mix the batter is ice cold and the batter is mixed at the last minute. Store the blossoms in the fridge, unwashed, until needed. They will be open when you pick them, but will close later.

16 courgette (baby marrow) flowers
8 medium courgettes (baby marrows)
10 green plum tomatoes
oil for deep-frying
140 g cake (plain) flour
1 egg yolk, beaten
250 ml ice-cold soda water
Maldon® sea salt

Wash and dry the flowers. Wash, dry and quarter the courgettes and green tomatoes. Heat the oil in a wok. Whisk the flour, egg yolk and soda water together until smooth. Dip each ingredient into the batter and allow to drip for 3 seconds, then place into the hot oil and fry until lightly golden brown. Drain well on paper towel and season with ground sea salt. Serve with Asian Tomato Salsa (page 32).

SERVES 8

Dill Coleslaw

1 large green cabbage

50 ml lemon juice

100 ml extra virgin olive oil

10 ml Dijon mustard

10 ml sugar

250 ml home-made mayonnaise (page 214)

150 ml fresh cream

100 ml plain yoghurt

1 large bunch fresh dill, finely chopped

Finely shred the cabbage and place in a large salad bowl. Whisk all the remaining ingredients together and pour over the cabbage. Toss well just before serving. Serve with Paprika Spatchcock Chicken (page 72) and Rustic 'Gogo' Chips (page 50).

SERVES 8–10

Vegetables

Vegetables play a huge part in our menus and our lives. We spend a good part of every day rooting around in the vegetable garden for ingredients and some of our cooking school courses focus on teaching people how to use ingredients they can grow themselves. Planning a menu for guests or a special family meal often happens while we are standing in the garden looking to see what's ready. The garden takes a lot of work and planning, but it's satisfying not to have to go to a supermarket every time you need a tomato, and challenging finding an alternative when there are no tomatoes in season.

Roasted Baby Corn with Whole Garlic

*This recipe is intended for fresh garlic, straight out of the ground.
If you use dried garlic, leave it to soak in hot water for 30–40 minutes
before roasting. This will hydrate the garlic and make it easier to roast.*

250 g whole baby corn

3 heads fresh garlic

30 ml extra virgin olive oil

Maldon® sea salt and freshly ground black pepper

1 bunch fresh thyme

Preheat the oven to 230 °C (450 °F, Gas Mark 8). Place the corn and
garlic in a roasting pan and drizzle with olive oil. Sprinkle with salt
and pepper. Place the bunch of fresh thyme on top and roast for
15–20 minutes until the corn is tender. Serve with crusty bread
smeared with the garlic.

SERVES 4

Creamed Spinach

70 g butter
70 g cake (plain) flour
750 ml milk
pinch of grated nutmeg
salt and freshly ground black pepper
1.5 kg spinach

Preheat the oven to 180 °C (350 °F, Gas Mark 4). Melt the butter in a small saucepan and whisk in the flour. Cook for 1–2 minutes, then remove from heat. Whisk in the milk until smooth. Return to the heat and cook until the mixture thickens and comes to the boil. Whisk continuously to prevent the formation of lumps. Remove from the heat and season with nutmeg, salt and pepper.

Remove the stalks from the spinach, then blanch the leaves in boiling water and refresh in cold water. Squeeze to remove excess water. Place half the blanched spinach and half the white sauce in a blender and blend together until smooth and creamy. Transfer to a serving dish and repeat the process. Check the seasoning and cover with tin foil. Heat in the oven for 15–20 minutes. Stir before serving.

SERVES 4–6

Roasted Hubbard Tart

1 x 23 cm shortcrust tart shell, baked blind (see Basics, page 216)

500 g Hubbard squash chunks

15 fresh sage leaves

45 ml olive oil

salt and freshly ground black pepper

100 g grated boerenkaas (you can substitute pecorino or
   a mature Cheddar cheese)

3 eggs

200 ml fresh cream

rocket leaves

balsamic vinegar

Preheat the oven to 230 °C (450 °F, Gas Mark 8). Make the filling by placing the Hubbard squash chunks in a roasting dish with 10 sage leaves. Drizzle with the olive oil and season with salt and pepper. Roast for 30–40 minutes until the squash is cooked and well coloured. Reduce the oven temperature to 180 °C (350 °F, Gas Mark 4).

   Sprinkle the grated boerenkaas onto the bottom of the pastry and top with the roasted squash chunks. Arrange the remaining sage leaves on top. Beat the eggs and cream together and season with salt and pepper. Pour over the tart filling and bake at 180 °C for 30 minutes until the tart is set to the touch. Serve with fresh rocket leaves drizzled with balsamic vinegar.

SERVES 6–8

Sweet Potato with Ginger, Orange & Chives

4 medium sweet potatoes

1 x thumb-sized piece of fresh root ginger

120 g softened butter

30 ml finely snipped chives

zest of 1 orange

salt and freshly ground black pepper

extra snipped chives to garnish

Preheat the oven to 190 °C (375 °F, Gas Mark 5). Clean and prick the skins of the sweet potatoes and place on a lightly oiled baking sheet. Bake for 40–60 minutes until the flesh is soft and the skin is crispy. While the potatoes are in the oven, peel and finely grate the ginger, then cream it together with the butter, chives, orange zest and seasoning. Halve the hot potatoes lengthways and arrange on a platter. Top each half with a generous helping of this lovely butter and sprinkle with extra fresh chives.

SERVES 4–6

Spinach & Feta Phyllo Tart

10 spring onions, finely sliced

175 g butter

500 g spinach, stalks removed and leaves roughly chopped

250 g feta cheese, crumbled

60 ml chopped fresh dill

45 ml chopped fresh Italian parsley

pinch of grated nutmeg

salt and freshly ground black pepper

6 sheets phyllo pastry

Preheat the oven to 220 °C (425 °F, Gas Mark 7). Sauté the spring onions in a large pan using 50 g of the butter. Add the spinach and let it wilt. Remove from the heat and add the feta, dill, parsley, nutmeg and seasoning. Set aside.

Melt the remaining butter. Line a greased 25 cm pie dish with a sheet of phyllo pastry. Brush this with the melted butter and put another sheet on top. Don't layer them directly over each other – set them at angles. Repeat this process until you have used all the phyllo, the edges of which are left protruding from the baking dish. Fill the pastry with the spinach mixture and fold in the flaps of phyllo to cover the filling. Give the top a last good brushing of butter before popping it into the oven for 45 minutes or until golden brown.

SERVES 4

Rustic 'Gogo' Chips

Gogo, my mother and granny to my children, formulated these chips as an alternative to the fried variety. We eat them all the time.

50 ml extra virgin olive oil
6 extra-large baking potatoes
30 ml wholewheat flour
Maldon® sea salt
freshly ground black pepper

Preheat the oven to 230 °C (450 °F, Gas Mark 8) – it must be very hot and up to full temperature before you start. Pour the olive oil into a large roasting pan and preheat in the oven for 3–4 minutes. In the meantime, wash the potatoes and slice lengthways into thickish wedges. Remove the roasting pan from the oven and add the potatoes to the hot oil. Season the chips with the flour, salt and pepper and return to the oven to bake for a further 45 minutes until golden brown and crispy. Shake the chips every now and then to loosen.

SERVES 6

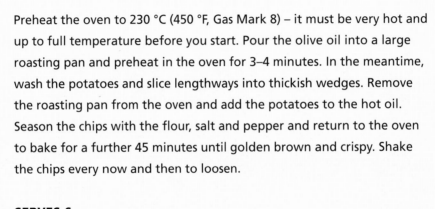

Ratatouille

This dish is delicious hot or cold with roast leg of lamb, poached eggs or on its own.

120 ml extra virgin olive oil

500 g fresh aubergines (brinjals), cut into chunks

5 large courgettes (baby marrows), cut into chunks

2 green peppers, seeded and roughly chopped

1 large onion, cut into eighths

1 x 400 g tin whole, peeled plum tomatoes, chopped

1 bay leaf

salt and freshly ground black pepper

2.5 ml cayenne pepper

3 cloves garlic, peeled and crushed

5 ml fresh thyme leaves

30 ml chopped fresh Italian parsley

8 fresh basil leaves, torn

Heat half the oil in a large, heavy-based pan and lightly brown the aubergines, courgettes, peppers and onion in batches. Transfer each batch to a large, heavy-based saucepan and pour over the remaining olive oil, tinned tomatoes and add the bay leaf. Season with salt, ground black pepper and cayenne pepper. Simmer, covered, for 30 minutes over medium heat, stirring often to ensure it doesn't burn. Stir in the garlic and thyme and cook for a further 20 minutes until thick. Serve sprinkled with the parsley and basil.

SERVES 8–10

Parsley Glazed Carrots

The carrots are best if they come straight from the earth. Make sure you clean them very well, especially at the top where the stalk is attached to the carrot.

20 baby carrots, with the green tips
45 g butter
10 ml honey
45 ml chopped fresh parsley

In a large pot of boiling salted water, blanch the baby carrots for 4–5 minutes, then rinse immediately and refresh in cold water. Melt the butter and honey in a large skillet, add the carrots and toss until coated and piping hot. Add the chopped parsley and serve.

SERVES 4

Roasted Fresh Garlic

This is a very simple recipe that deserves a mention here because it is the best thing to do with garlic fresh from the garden. You can serve it with roasts and so on, but the best way to enjoy it is with buttered toast.

3 heads fresh garlic
15 ml olive oil
Maldon® sea salt and freshly ground black pepper

Preheat the oven to 180 °C (350 °F, Gas Mark 4). Cut each head of garlic in half horizontally and lay them skin side down in a roasting dish. Drizzle with olive oil and season with salt and pepper, then roast for 25–30 minutes until the skin is browning and the cloves are soft and juicy.

SERVES 2–4

Pommes Alumette

8 medium potatoes
2 litres sunflower oil
salt and freshly ground black pepper

Peel the potatoes and place in a large bowl of water. Using a mandolin with the smallest chip cutter, secure the hand protector to each potato and slice in an up-and-down movement. The result should be a matchstick-sized chip. When cut, place the chips in another bowl of water until all the potatoes are done.

   Heat the oil in a wok, deep-fryer or a large, heavy-based pot on high until very hot. While the oil is heating, drain the chips and dry thoroughly on kitchen towels. Water and oil do not react well so the chips must be really dry, otherwise the oil will bubble over when the chips are added. When the oil is very hot, add the cut chips a handful at a time. Stir with a slotted spoon and cook until crispy and golden. Repeat this in batches. Drain the cooked chips on paper towel, season and serve on a large platter. If necessary, they can be reheated in the oven for 10 minutes at 200 °C (400 °F, Gas Mark 6).

SERVES 6

Spinach & Mushroom Rotolo

FILLING	15 ml olive oil
45 g butter	250 g button mushrooms, sliced
45 g cake (plain) flour	600 ml tomato concassée (page 217)
250 ml milk	Parmesan cheese shavings
pinch of grated nutmeg	
salt and freshly ground black pepper	PASTA
500 g spinach, stalks removed	400 g cake (plain) flour
150 g feta cheese, crumbled	4 eggs
12 spring onions, chopped	

To make the filling, melt the butter in a small saucepan, add the flour and cook for 1 minute. Pour in the milk and whisk until the mixture thickens and comes to the boil. Season with the nutmeg, salt and pepper. Chop the spinach, place in a blender with the white sauce and blend. Transfer to a bowl and add the feta and spring onions. Heat the olive oil in a small pan and fry the mushrooms until cooked. Set aside.

Make the pasta by following the directions laid out on page 218. Roll out the pasta in a pasta machine, using gradually thinner settings until the final sheets are rolled on the finest setting. Lay the pasta sheets, brushed with a little water, on top of a lightly floured tea towel to form a rectangle with 5 cm of the towel exposed on each edge. Spread the filling over the pasta and scatter mushrooms on top. Roll up the rotolo along the longest length using the tea towel and tuck in the exposed ends. Secure with string at 10 cm intervals. Place in a fish kettle (poaching pan) filled halfway with boiling salted water and boil, covered, for 45–50 minutes. Remove and cool for 5–10 minutes, then unwrap, slice and arrange on six small plates with tomato concassée and Parmesan shavings.

SERVES 6

58

Roasted Asparagus

If you can't get white asparagus just use green.

600 g green asparagus

400 g white asparagus

50 ml olive oil

4 cloves garlic, peeled and sliced

Maldon® sea salt and freshly ground black pepper

100 g calamata olives

10 fresh basil leaves

Preheat the oven to 230 °C (450 °F, Gas Mark 8). Cut off the end of each asparagus and place the spears in a colander. Wash and allow to drip-dry. Transfer to a large roasting pan, drizzle with the olive oil and scatter the garlic slices over the top. Shake the pan to ensure all the asparagus spears are coated. Season with salt and pepper and roast in the hot oven for 10–12 minutes. Be careful not to overcook (it all depends on the thickness of the asparagus). Remove from the oven and add the olives and torn basil leaves just before serving.

SERVES 6–8

Cauliflower Mustard Cheese

2 heads cauliflower

45 g butter

45 g cake (plain) flour

750 ml milk

10 ml wholegrain mustard

2.5 ml grated nutmeg

salt and freshly ground black pepper

50 g grated Parmesan cheese

Preheat the oven to 180 °C (350 °F, Gas Mark 4). Place a large pot of water over high heat and bring to the boil. Blanch the whole heads of cauliflower for 15 minutes. Remove from heat and refresh in iced water. Drain and set aside.

To make the mustard sauce, melt the butter in a medium saucepan and add the flour, whisking all the time. Add the milk and bring to the boil, whisking constantly to prevent lumps. When the mixture comes to the boil, add the mustard, nutmeg and salt and pepper to taste. Place the blanched cauliflower heads (leave them whole) in an ovenproof dish and smother in the sauce. Sprinkle with the grated cheese and bake in the oven for 30–40 minutes until soft and gooey.

SERVES 6–8

French Onion Soup

This is a great main course for winter and for vegetarians. Vegetarians can replace the bacon with 2.5 ml smoked paprika and use vegetable stock instead of chicken or beef.

4 large onions, thinly sliced

45 g butter

2 rashers streaky bacon

2 cloves garlic, peeled and crushed

1 sprig fresh thyme

30 ml cake (plain) flour

2 litres beef or chicken stock

100 ml brandy

salt and freshly ground black pepper

8 thick slices French bread

100 ml olive oil

Sauté the onions in the butter together with the bacon rashers, garlic and thyme until the onions are soft. Sprinkle the flour over the onion mixture and stir well. Slowly pour in the stock and bring to the boil, stirring constantly. Reduce the heat and simmer for 45 minutes. Just before serving, remove the bacon rashers, then add the brandy, salt and black pepper to the soup. Shallow-fry the slices of bread in the olive oil until golden brown and serve with the hot soup.

SERVES 8

Potato Dauphinois

The central feature of this dish, apart from using our own potatoes, is our fresh farm cream. A good thick store-bought cream will do, but it just isn't the same.

500 ml milk
500 ml fresh cream
4 cloves garlic
1.5 kg potatoes, peeled and thinly sliced (use a mandolin if you have one)
salt and freshly ground black pepper
30 ml chopped fresh parsley

Preheat the oven to 180 °C (350 °F, Gas Mark 4). Bring the milk, cream and garlic to the boil in a large saucepan. Add the potato slices to the milk mixture, coating the slices as thoroughly as possible without breaking them. Season with salt and pepper and bring to the boil again. Remove from the heat and transfer all the ingredients from the saucepan to a baking dish. Pop into the oven for 35–45 minutes until the top is well browned. Garnish with the parsley and serve.

SERVES 6

French Potato Pie

This simple but delicious classic French pie makes an easy and substantial lunch served with a fresh garden salad. The secret to well-risen pastry is a sharp knife for trimming the edges before baking. Crispy pastry is all about using an enamel pie dish.

450 g waxy potatoes (do not peel)
6 spring onions, sliced
2 cloves garlic, peeled and finely chopped
30 ml chopped fresh flat-leaf parsley
salt and freshly ground black pepper
2 x 400 g ready-to-roll puff pastry
1 large egg, beaten
200 ml crème fraîche or double sour cream

Preheat the oven to 230 °C (450 °F, Gas Mark 8). Slice the potatoes very thinly into a bowl and mix with the spring onions, garlic, parsley and some salt and pepper. Roll out the first sheet of pastry on a lightly floured surface and use it to line a 24 cm enamel pie dish. Trim the edges and keep the offcuts for a design on the top of the pie. Layer the potato slices in the pastry case and cover with the other rolled pastry. Brush the top with egg wash and, using the offcuts, create a latticework or leaves on the top.

Bake the pie in the hot oven for 15 minutes, then reduce the heat to 200 °C (400 °F, Gas Mark 6) and cook for a further 25 minutes until the potatoes are soft. Remove from the oven and carefully lift off the top of the pie. Pour the crème fraîche into the pie, replace the pastry lid and bake for another 8–10 minutes. Serve thick wedges of potato pie with a garden salad.

SERVES 6–8

66

Poultry
& Game Birds

We eat a lot of chicken, not only for health reasons, but because it is a convenient source of meat when you live on a farm. We keep chickens for eggs and raise a few birds for their meat every now and then, preferring traditional breeds to fast-growing broilers. We also have access to wild duck and guinea fowl thanks to the bird hunters in the area, so we've included some of our favourite recipes here. Game birds feature heavily on the menus for our American guests, and the Wild Duck à la Colette is an absolute institution with them. Also featured is an often-requested recipe for Chowed Chicken that Camilla picked up when she worked with renowned Chinese chef Nancy Cox in San Francisco.

Chicken Curry with Baby Aubergines

12 chicken thighs (skin on)

2 medium onions, chopped

4 cloves garlic, peeled and crushed

15 ml crushed fresh ginger

20 ml sunflower oil

45 ml chopped curry leaves

½ bunch chopped fresh coriander

5 ml mustard seeds

5 ml coriander seeds

5 ml fennel seeds

2 ml turmeric

5 ml ground cumin

1 stick cinnamon

30 ml freshly mixed garam masala

800 g peeled and chopped tomatoes

250 ml chicken stock

salt and sugar

20 baby aubergines (brinjals), halved

Preheat the oven to 180 °C (350 °F, Gas Mark 4). Heat a large, deep pan (don't add oil) and brown the thighs on both sides, starting with the skin side down. Do this in batches. Remove the browned thighs and place in an ovenproof casserole. Discard any excess fat from the pan, then fry the onions, garlic and ginger in the sunflower oil. Add the curry leaves, fresh coriander and all the spices. Add the tomatoes and stock and season with salt and sugar to taste. Bring to the boil and add the aubergines. Pour the sauce over the chicken pieces and cover with tin foil or a lid. Bake in the oven for 1½ hours. Serve with jasmine rice.

SERVES 6–8

Paprika Spatchcock Chicken

2 medium chickens, split down the backbone

MARINADE
100 ml olive oil
4 large lemons
10 ml smoked paprika
10 ml dried oregano
salt and freshly ground black pepper

Prepare a barbecue (braai) or preheat the oven to 200 °C (400 °C, Gas Mark 6). Place the chickens in a large roasting pan. Mix all the marinade ingredients together and massage into the chicken. Leave to marinate in a cool spot for 3–4 hours. If you choose to cook the chickens on the barbecue, it is vital to have very hot coals. Chargrill the chickens, starting bone side down on the grill. The cooking process takes about 20 minutes, depending on the size of the chickens and the temperature of the coals. If using the oven, cook the chickens for 45 minutes. Serve with Dill Coleslaw (page 39) and Mealie Bread (pages 149 or 150).

SERVES 8–10

Granny's Baked Chicken Stuffing

1 onion, quartered

4 rashers bacon

125 g chicken livers

½ loaf stale brown bread, crumbled

45 ml chopped fresh parsley

1 egg

125 ml olive oil

100 ml fresh cream

salt and freshly ground black pepper

45 g butter

Preheat the oven to 180 °C (350 °F, Gas Mark 4). Put the onion, bacon, chicken livers, bread and parsley through a mincer (hand or electric) and mix together with the egg, olive oil and cream in the bowl that catches the ingredients. Season with salt and pepper. Spoon into a lightly buttered ovenproof dish and dot the top with butter. Bake for 30 minutes until golden brown and the edges are crispy. Serve with roast chicken.

SERVES 6

Spicy Chicken Liver & Avocado Sandwich

2 Portuguese rolls

butter

15 ml olive oil

4 spring onions, finely sliced

250 g chicken livers

4 ml Tabasco® sauce

salt and freshly ground black pepper

1 ripe avocado, sliced

8 rashers bacon, fried or grilled until crispy

Halve and butter the rolls. Heat the olive oil in a small skillet and sauté the spring onions. Add the chicken livers and Tabasco®. Season with salt and pepper and continue to cook for a further 6–8 minutes until the livers are cooked through. When done, pile the filling onto half of each roll, followed by avocado slices and crispy bacon rashers.

SERVES 2

Grilled Chicken Breasts with Sage Butter

4 skinless chicken breast fillets
50 ml olive oil
juice of 1 lemon
olive oil for frying
60 g butter
20 fresh sage leaves

Marinate the chicken breasts in the olive oil and lemon juice for 1–2 hours.
   Preheat the oven to 180 °C (350 °F, Gas Mark 4). Heat a large frying pan over medium heat and add some olive oil. Fry the chicken breasts until browned on both sides, then place in a baking dish and bake in the oven for 5–7 minutes. While the chicken is in the oven, return the frying pan to the stove and melt the butter. Add the sage and cook until the leaves are dark brown and crispy. Slice the chicken breasts, spoon some sage butter over each one and serve with Creamed Spinach (page 44) and Rustic 'Gogo' Chips (page 50).

SERVES 4

Chowed Chicken with Black Beans

This is a favourite of all serious Chinese food freaks and if the chicken is not overcooked, the result will be spectacular. It might look like a lot of work, but it isn't.

1 x 1.5 kg chicken, chopped into bite-size pieces

60 ml peanut oil

3 cloves garlic, peeled and crushed

1 yellow onion, roughly chopped

45 ml fermented black beans (dowsee – available from Chinese supermarkets or speciality food stores), rinsed in water and mashed with 30 ml rice wine

2 green peppers, julienned

MARINADE

15 ml peanut oil

30 ml light soy sauce

30 ml cornflour

1 egg white

2.5 ml salt

SAUCE

15 ml light soy sauce

30 ml dry sherry or rice wine

250 ml chicken stock

5 ml brown sugar

Whisk together all the ingredients for the marinade and pour over the chicken pieces. Leave to marinate for 15 minutes. Drain the marinade from the chicken and reserve. Heat a wok and add 30 ml of the peanut oil until smoking hot. Brown the chicken pieces very well, then remove and set aside. Discard the oil in the wok. Heat the wok again, add the remaining 30 ml oil and stir-fry the garlic for a moment. Add the onion and black beans and cook for 1 minute. Add the green peppers. Return the chicken to the wok along with the reserved marinade. Add all the ingredients for the sauce and stir well. Cover and simmer for about 20 minutes until the chicken is tender but not overcooked. Serve with boiled white rice and steamed broccoli.

SERVES 6

78

Lemon & Leek Chicken Thighs

8 leeks, roughly chopped

6 carrots, roughly chopped

8 chicken thighs (skin on)

8 cloves garlic, unpeeled

4 bay leaves

3 sprigs fresh thyme

30 ml olive oil

juice of 1 lemon

250 ml dry white wine

salt and freshly ground black pepper

Preheat the oven to 180 °C (350 °F, Gas Mark 4). Place the leeks and carrots on the bottom of a roasting pan. Arrange the chicken pieces, garlic, bay leaves and thyme on top. Drizzle the olive oil, lemon juice and wine over all the ingredients. Season with salt and pepper, cover with tin foil and bake in the oven for 45 minutes. Remove the tin foil, increase the oven temperature to 220 °C (425 °F, Gas Mark 7) and cook for a further 15 minutes until the chicken skin is golden brown and crispy. Serve with Baked Polenta (page 212).

SERVES 4

Braised Guinea Fowl Legs & Thighs

10 guinea fowl legs with thighs attached

250 ml olive oil

handful of fresh thyme sprigs

handful of fresh marjoram (stalks and all)

salt and freshly ground black pepper

125 ml dry sherry

250 ml dry white wine

Marinate the guinea fowl in 125 ml of the olive oil overnight in the refrigerator. Bring back to room temperature before cooking.

Preheat the oven to 200 °C (400 °F, Gas Mark 6). Heat a non-stick frying pan and brown the guinea fowl on both sides until golden in colour. Line the bottom of a large roasting dish with half the thyme and half the marjoram. Place the guinea fowl on top, making sure not to overlap the pieces. Season with salt and pepper and cover with the remaining herbs. Pour over the remaining olive oil, the sherry and the white wine. Cover with tin foil and bake for 1½–2 hours. Serve with Artichoke Mash (page 215), steamed broccoli and Crab Apple Jelly (page 160).

SERVES 6–8

Slow Roast Chicken with Garlic, Lemon & Sage

30 ml olive oil
10 chicken thighs (skin on)
salt and freshly ground black pepper
2 lemons, quartered
10 cloves garlic, unpeeled
10 fresh sage leaves
200 ml dry white wine

Preheat the oven to 140 °C (275 °F, Gas Mark 1). Heat the olive oil in
a large skillet and brown the seasoned chicken pieces on both sides,
starting skin side down. Transfer to a large roasting pan or skillet and
arrange the lemons, garlic and sage around the chicken. Pour over the
white wine and cover the roasting pan with tin foil. Roast in the oven
for 1 hour. Remove the tin foil and increase the oven temperature to
220 °C (425 °F, Gas Mark 7). Return the uncovered chicken to the oven
and roast for a further 20 minutes until golden brown. Serve with
Potato Dauphinois (page 65) and steamed broccoli.

SERVES 6–8

Wild Duck à la Colette

You'll need 10 wild yellow-billed ducks, plucked and innards removed. Cook the legs and breasts separately, as they require different attention.

DUCK STOCK

4 duck carcasses

Preheat the oven to 230 °C (450 °F, Gas Mark 8) and brown the carcasses for 30–40 minutes. Transfer to a stockpot and cover with at least 2 litres cold water. Bring to the boil, then reduce heat and simmer for 3 hours to obtain a good-coloured stock. Strain the stock.

DUCK LEGS

20 duck legs with thighs attached

15 ml peanut oil

1 medium onion, sliced

3 cloves garlic, peeled and crushed

30 ml crushed fresh ginger

60 ml light soy sauce

60 ml black rice vinegar

5 ml brown sugar

1.5 litres duck stock

Preheat the oven to 180 °C (350 °F, Gas Mark 4). In a very hot pan, brown the duck on both sides in the peanut oil. Transfer to a heavy-based, stainless steel, ovenproof saucepan. Sauté the onion in the remaining oil and add the garlic and ginger. Cook for 1 minute, then add the soy sauce, black vinegar and sugar and deglaze the pan with 125 ml of the duck stock. Pour this sauce over the duck legs, then add the remaining stock to cover the legs completely. Cover the saucepan and place in the

84

oven for 2–3 hours until very tender. Check periodically to ensure there is enough liquid and that the legs are not becoming overcooked. The cooking time depends on the age of the birds and cannot be precisely given. Set aside until needed, then reheat at 180 °C for 20 minutes.

DUCK BREASTS

These are cooked rare with the skin on. When cooked, the skin is removed and the flesh sliced. This can be a bloody affair, but the results are worth it, so persevere. Make sure the sauce is boiling hot just before serving.

45 ml sugar

45 ml red wine vinegar

45 ml fresh orange juice

5 ml orange zest

250 ml duck stock

250 ml sauce from the duck legs

10 ml cornflour dissolved in a little water

16 duck breasts

watercress to garnish

Caramelize the sugar in a saucepan over medium heat. Add the vinegar and dissolve the sugar, then add the orange juice, zest, stock and duck leg sauce. Bring to the boil and thicken with cornflour. Remove from heat and set aside. Fifteen minutes before dinner, preheat the oven to 230 °C (450 °F, Gas Mark 8) and roast the breasts skin side up for exactly 7 minutes. With a very sharp knife, remove and discard the skin and slice each breast thinly. Place on a serving platter. Bring the orange sauce back to the boil and pour over the sliced meat just before serving. Arrange the legs around the sides of the platter and garnish with watercress. Serve with snow peas, baby corn and brown and wild rice.

SERVES 8–10

Simple Roast Chicken

The secret to a moist roast chicken is not to overcook it. The tendency to do this comes from the fear of salmonella, but as long as you raise the temperature above 80 °C (175 °F) right through the bird during the cooking process – which you will by roasting it – this is not a problem. It is a sin to dry out a fresh farm bird, as you want to bring out the succulence and flavour.

1 farm or free-range chicken
3 cloves garlic, peeled and crushed
freshly ground sea salt and black pepper
30 g butter

Preheat the oven to 200 °C (400 °F, Gas Mark 6). Wash the chicken and pat it dry. Place the chicken in a roasting dish, smear with the garlic, season with salt and pepper and spread half the butter over each breast. Roast for 45–60 minutes until the skin is crispy and the chicken is cooked. An average-sized chicken of 1.5 kg should not take more than 1 hour to cook. A simple test to see when the chicken is cooked is to slip a knife between the thigh and the body and see if there is any blood. If not, then the bird is cooked. Serve with Roasted Figs (page 173).

SERVES 4

Meat

We're very lucky to be able to raise our own cattle and pigs because meat is an expensive commodity. In particular, we raise pigs for the kitchen because they eat all the organic leavings from the garden and from kitchen preparation – all the greens and offcuts and peels. Our pigs get no offal or additives, and you really can taste this in the flesh. The difference between mass-produced and organic or green-reared pigs is quite remarkable. It's good to know where your meat came from and – in our case – how it was reared. This is true of everything from pigs to cattle and chickens. Rather pay a little more and know that the animals were raised in a humane way with sensible and sensitive inputs – it makes cooking and eating the meat much more of a privilege.

Oxtail

3.5 kg oxtail, excess fat removed
125 ml cake (plain) flour, seasoned with salt and
freshly ground black pepper
60 ml olive oil
1 kg red onions, roughly chopped
5 fresh bay leaves
10 juniper berries
6 cloves garlic, peeled and crushed
750 ml red wine
500 ml beef stock
500 g peas
8 medium carrots, sliced
1 large bunch fresh parsley, chopped

Preheat the oven to 180 °C (350 °F, Gas Mark 4). Roll each oxtail joint in
the seasoned flour and set aside. Heat the oil in a large pan and brown
the oxtail on both sides in batches. This is an important process, as
browning will give colour to the dish as well as seal in the juices. Once
all the meat is browned, transfer it to a large casserole dish.

   Heat a little more olive oil in the pan if needed and sauté the onions,
bay leaves, juniper berries and garlic. Add the red wine and season. Pour
this over the meat and add the beef stock. The meat should be covered
in liquid. Cover with a lid and place in the oven for 4–5 hours until the
meat is tender. (The older the oxtail the longer it will take to cook.)
Blanch the peas in a separate pot of boiling water. Do the same to the
sliced carrots and add to the cooked oxtail with the chopped parsley just
before serving. You can also serve the peas and carrots separately, with
Mashed Potatoes (page 215) or Parsley Couscous (page 213).

SERVES 6–8

Roast Pork Belly

The secret to crackling is well-scored rind and a very hot oven to start the cooking process. Remember, the less fat, the higher the grade of pork.

1 whole pork belly, rind on
Maldon® sea salt
freshly ground black pepper
10 ml fennel seeds

Preheat the oven to 230 °C (450 °F, Gas Mark 8). Score the rind with a very sharp knife, with cuts about 1 cm apart. Place the roast on an oven rack over a roasting pan and season with the sea salt. Roast for 30 minutes until the skin is well crackled. Remove the roast and reduce the oven temperature to 140 °C (275 °F, Gas Mark 1). Sprinkle the roast with the pepper and fennel seeds and cook for a further 1½ hours until beautifully tender. Serve with roast sweet potatoes and red cabbage or roast potatoes and a salad.

SERVES 4–6

Game Pie

2 kg bush pig loin (or any other venison), cut into cubes

30 g butter

15 ml olive oil

2 onions, sliced

100 ml dry sherry

1.5 litres game stock (page 211)

salt and freshly ground black pepper

500 g button mushrooms, sliced

1 bunch fresh parsley, chopped

500 g ready-to-roll puff pastry

1 egg, beaten

Preheat the oven to 180 °C (350 °F, Gas Mark 4). Brown the meat in a large dry pan, then transfer to a casserole. Heat the butter and olive oil, sauté the onions, then deglaze the pan with sherry. Pour the mixture over the meat and add the stock – the liquid must cover the meat. Season with salt and pepper and cover with a lid. Cook in the oven for 1½–2 hours until the meat is tender. Remove the meat with a slotted spoon and set aside. Transfer the sauce to a saucepan and thicken with roux (mixture of equal parts butter and flour). Fry the mushrooms in a little olive oil, then add together with the meat and parsley to the thickened sauce. Transfer to a pie dish and leave to cool.

Roll out the pastry and trim the edges with a sharp knife. Cover the filling with the pastry and crimp the edges with a fork. Garnish with pastry shapes and make two holes in the pastry to allow the steam to escape. Heat the oven to 220 °C (425 °F, Gas Mark 7). Brush the pastry with egg and bake the pie for 30–45 minutes until golden brown.

SERVES 8–10

Perfect Pork Ribs

3.5 kg fresh pork ribs
45 ml honey

MARINADE
150 ml tomato sauce
150 ml light soy sauce
40 ml hoisin sauce
50 ml olive oil
50 ml rice wine vinegar
75 g fresh ginger, crushed
8 cloves garlic, crushed
45 ml brown sugar

Place the ribs in a large, non-metallic bowl. Mix all the marinade
ingredients together and pour over the ribs. Marinate overnight
in the refrigerator.

Preheat the oven to 180 °C (350 °F, Gas Mark 4). Divide the ribs
between two large roasting pans and cover with tin foil. Roast in
the oven for 45–60 minutes until soft and tender. Place the ribs over
a bed of coals or under a grill to give them colour (we prefer coals for
the smoky flavour). Mix 45 ml of the cooking liquid in the pan with
the honey and use as a basting for the ribs.

SERVES 6

Waterblommetjie Bredie

1 kg lamb neck

30 ml olive oil

2 medium onions, sliced

1 red chilli, seeded and chopped

3 cloves garlic, peeled and sliced

300 g sorrel

12–15 waterblommetjies

250 ml dry white wine

125 ml water

salt and freshly ground black pepper

12 baby potatoes

Preheat the oven to 180 °C (350 °F, Gas Mark 4). Snip the neck edges at the top to prevent them from curling during cooking. Heat the olive oil in a pan and brown the lamb on both sides. Remove from the pan and place in an ovenproof casserole.

In the same pan, sauté the onions, then add the chilli and garlic and cook for a further 2 minutes. Add the sorrel, waterblommetjies, white wine and water. Season with salt and pepper. Pour the sauce over the meat and cover the casserole. Cook in the oven for 1½ hours, adding a little water if needed during the cooking process. Add the potatoes and cook until the potatoes are just done – about 25 minutes. Add more seasoning if necessary. The bredie should be soft and tender. Serve with yellow rice and raisins.

SERVES 4

Bobotie

*This recipe improves with age so make it the day before serving.
It can be reheated in the oven at 180 °C (350 °F, Gas Mark 4) for
about 20 minutes or until heated through.*

1 large onion, quartered	1 kg minced lamb or beef
1 thumb-sized piece fresh ginger, peeled	15 ml tomato paste
	15 ml apricot jam
2 cloves garlic, peeled	60 ml lemon juice
5 whole cloves	15 ml cake (plain) flour
15 ml cumin seeds	1 thick slice white bread
15 ml turmeric	250 ml milk
3 cardamom pods	4 eggs
25 ml medium curry powder	3 drops almond essence
½ stick cinnamon	2.5 ml grated nutmeg
30 ml sunflower oil	6 bay leaves

Preheat the oven to 160 °C (325 °F, Gas Mark 3). In a food processor
blend together the onion, ginger, garlic, cloves, cumin seeds, turmeric,
cardamom, curry powder and cinnamon until chopped. Heat the oil in a
pan and add the blended ingredients. Fry until the onion is soft, then
remove from the heat and put into a large bowl. Add the mince, tomato
paste, apricot jam, lemon juice and flour. In a separate bowl, soak the
bread in the milk. Squeeze out the bread and add to the above
ingredients and mix very well. Pack the meat mixture into a shallow,
round or 30 x 20 cm rectangular casserole dish. Beat the eggs into the
remaining milk, add almond essence and nutmeg and pour over the
meat. Arrange the bay leaves on top and bake for 1 hour until firm to
the touch. Serve with yellow rice.

SERVES 6–8

French Roast Whole Fillet

1.3 kg beef fillet, membrane removed

15 ml whole grain mustard

30 ml coarsely ground black pepper

2 sprigs fresh rosemary

Preheat the oven to 230 °C (450 °F, Gas Mark 8). Place the fillet in a shallow roasting pan. Smear the mustard over the top of the fillet and sprinkle over the black pepper to form a crust. Strip the leaves from the rosemary and sprinkle over the meat. Roast in the oven for 20–25 minutes until the meat is firm to the touch; this will give you a rare to medium-rare fillet. Set aside to rest for 15 minutes before serving. Serve with Chilli Aïoli (page 214) or Red Wine Sauce (page 211).

SERVES 4–6

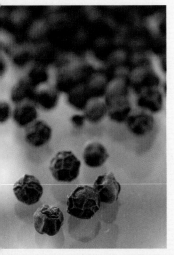

Meat Loaf

1 x 410 g tin tomato purée (passata)

400 g minced topside

100 g minced pork

40 g oats

1 small onion, finely chopped

2 cloves garlic, peeled and crushed

60 g Parmesan cheese, grated

30 ml chopped fresh Italian parsley

100 ml red wine

5 ml sugar

7.5 ml salt

2.5 ml freshly ground black pepper

1 egg

bay leaves to garnish (optional)

Preheat the oven to 180 °C (350 °F, Gas Mark 4). In a large bowl, combine half the tin of tomato purée with the remaining ingredients and mix well. Lightly grease a 25 x 10 cm loaf tin and shape the mixture into it. Pour the remaining tomato purée over the loaf and bake for 1 hour. Garnish with the bay leaves (if using) and serve hot or cold with pickles and home-made bread.

SERVES 6–8

102

Slow Roast Brisket

The brisket is even more delicious when cooked in a wood-fired oven, as the smoky flavour adds to the richness of this simple roast.

2.5 kg brisket
salt and freshly ground black pepper
12–15 leeks, halved lengthways
15–20 fresh bay leaves (about 2 sprigs)
3 whole heads garlic, tops removed

Preheat the oven to 230 °C (450 °F, Gas Mark 8). Score the fat on the top of the roast in a crisscross pattern and rub the entire surface with salt and pepper. Place the halved leeks, bay leaves and garlic on the base of a large roasting pan. Position the seasoned roast on top and place in the oven to seal the meat very well. This will take a good 20–30 minutes. Remove the roast from the oven and reduce the heat to 150–140 °C (300–275 °F, Gas Mark 2 or 1). Cover the roast with a double layer of tin foil and return to the oven for at least 6–8 hours.

SERVES 8

Teriyaki Leg of Lamb

1.8–2 kg leg of lamb, deboned and butterflied

MARINADE
65 ml dark soy sauce
65 ml sake
30 ml Chinese rice wine
15 ml sugar
1 thumb-sized piece fresh ginger, crushed
4 cloves garlic, crushed
45 ml tomato ketchup

Mix all the marinade ingredients together. Place the lamb in a non-metallic bowl, pour the marinade over the lamb and marinate overnight, covered and in the refrigerator.

Preheat the oven to 200 °C (400 °F, Gas Mark 6). Transfer the lamb to a roasting pan and roast for 40–45 minutes until just pink. Set aside to rest for 15 minutes, then slice and arrange on a serving platter. Serve with Roasted Asparagus (page 60) and Parsley Couscous (page 213).

SERVES 6–8

Meatballs in Tomato Sauce

TOMATO SAUCE	MEATBALLS
1 small onion, finely chopped	500 g minced beef
60 ml olive oil	30 ml finely chopped onion
350 ml tomato purée (passata)	2 cloves garlic, peeled and crushed
– we make ours from our own	45 ml fresh breadcrumbs
tomatoes, straining out the seeds	5 ml chopped fresh mint
before pulping and freezing	2.5 ml dried oregano
15 ml red wine vinegar	4 ml ground allspice
5 ml smoked paprika	salt and freshly ground black pepper
2.5 ml ground cinnamon	1 egg, lightly beaten
2.5 ml ground cloves	cake (plain) flour
5 ml sugar	30 g butter
salt and freshly ground black pepper	30 ml olive oil

Make the sauce first. Sauté the onion in the olive oil in a saucepan until
soft. Add the tomato purée, vinegar, paprika, cinnamon, cloves, sugar
and salt and pepper to taste. Cook, covered, over medium heat for
about 15 minutes, stirring often.

To make the meatballs, mix the mince with the onion, garlic and
breadcrumbs. Add the herbs, allspice and salt and pepper. Mix in the
egg until thoroughly combined. Flour your hands and shape the meat
mixture into 16 medium meatballs. Heat the butter and olive oil in
a large frying pan and brown the meatballs on all sides. Transfer the
meatballs to the pot of tomato sauce and simmer for 10–15 minutes.
Stir once in a while to ensure even cooking.

SERVES 4

Boerewors (Farmer's Sausage)

The sausage casings used to make the boerewors can be frozen and taken out as required. Simply sprinkle with a little salt to preserve during the freezing process. One sausage casing usually makes 1.5–2 kg of sausage. Remember that once hydrated (soaked) the casings must be discarded if not used.

75 ml coriander seeds

30 ml whole allspice (pimento)

45 ml salt

30 ml freshly ground black pepper

90 ml biltong spice (ask your butcher)

6 kg minced beef

2 kg minced fatty pork

6 dehydrated sausage casings

Place the coriander and allspice in a dry pan and roast the spices evenly. Transfer to a spice grinder and grind finely. Mix this together with the remaining seasonings. In a large bowl, mix together the beef mince, pork mince and all the seasoning until they are well combined. Place the sausage casings in cold water to hydrate for at least 30 minutes. Slip the casing over the funnel part of a sausage maker and gently ease the meat into the casing until you have a roll of sausage. Knot the ends. The boerewors can be frozen for 2 months or used immediately. The best way to cook wors is to barbecue (braai) it on an open fire.

MAKES ABOUT 6 KG

Home-made Pork Sausages

Make friends with your local butcher and get him to help you with meat selection, deboning or rinding joints and setting aside bits like the cheeks.

900 g deboned, rinded pork shoulder	10 ml whole grain mustard
4 pigs' cheeks	5 ml Worcestershire sauce
225 g rinded pork back fat	1 egg, beaten
2 onions, finely chopped	2 slices white bread, crumbed
30 g butter	salt and freshly ground black pepper
2.5 ml chopped fresh thyme	4 m sausage casing, soaked in cold
5 ml chopped fresh sage	water for at least 30 minutes
2 cloves garlic, peeled and crushed	

Pass the shoulder, cheeks and back fat through a mincer. In a pan over medium heat, sauté the onions in the butter with the herbs and garlic. Remove from the heat and leave to cool. Mix the cooled onion mixture into the minced meat, and add the mustard, Worcestershire sauce, egg, breadcrumbs and salt and pepper. Slip the soaked sausage casing onto the tube of a sausage maker. Feed the meat mixture into the casing about 20 cm at a time, knotting in between, until all the mixture is used up. Rest the sausages for 30 minutes in the refrigerator before cooking over high heat for about 10 minutes until browned on all sides. Serve either with breakfast or with Mashed Potatoes (page 215) and Red Wine Onion Marmalade (page 213).

MAKES ABOUT 16 SAUSAGES

Salami

Once you have mastered this basic cooked salami recipe, you can experiment with different ingredients such as garlic or green peppercorns to further enhance the flavour.

6 kg minced beef

4 kg minced fatty pork

250 g cooked salami spice (available from your butcher)

75 g non-iodated salt

1.5 litres water

4 salami casings (use porous casings if you want to smoke the salami)

Mix the beef and pork mince together in a large bowl – your hands are the best tools here, but a wooden spoon will do. Dissolve the spice and the salt in the water, then add it to the meat. Mix this until all the liquid is absorbed and the mince has a paste-like quality.

Pack the meat into the casings, one at a time, making sure to tamp it down and allowing as little air as possible into the salami. Tie the salamis off with string, then place them in a *bain-marie*. The water in the *bain-marie* should never boil, but you should gradually raise the temperature at the centre of each salami to 70 °C (160 °F) – test with a meat thermometer. Once the goal temperature is reached, the salamis should be plunged straight into cold water to cool before smoking or refrigerating. Whether you smoke them or not, salami should hang for 2 weeks before use.

MAKES 4 X 2.5 KG SALAMIS

Fish & Seafood

The Comins men are keen fishermen who have fished everywhere from the local river to Kenya, Mozambique and Kosi Bay. We live far from the sea, but have access to fresh fish thanks to their expeditions. Trevor is also a lifelong prawn addict, and as these little crustaceans freeze so well, there's no reason why we can't enjoy them on the farm. Jason learned to cook fish in County Cork in Ireland and always quips 'long time no sea' when we haul the prawns out of the freezer. Remember, it is better to eat fish frozen fresh on the spot than fresh fish that was caught a few days ago.

Caviar Pâté

8 hard-boiled eggs

45 g softened butter

salt and freshly ground black pepper

500 ml sour cream

1 onion, finely chopped

1 x 100 g jar red lumpfish caviar

1 x 100 g jar black lumpfish caviar

30 ml chopped fresh Italian parsley

Peel the eggs and mash together with the soft butter and seasoning. Pack this mixture firmly into an attractive, shallow serving dish. Beat the cream until thick, then add the onion and season once again. Spoon and spread this on top of the egg mixture and refrigerate until just before the guests arrive. Before serving, dollop teaspoonfuls of the lumpfish caviar in a design on the cream topping and sprinkle with parsley. Serve with hot bagels or home-made bread.

SERVES 6

Prawn Sandwich with Dill Mayonnaise

15 ml butter

10 prawns, peeled and deveined

1 clove garlic, crushed

salt and freshly ground black pepper

15 ml chopped fresh dill

20 ml mayonnaise

1 wholewheat roll

4 thick slices cucumber

1 lime

Melt the butter in a pan and fry the prawns and garlic for 4–5 minutes until cooked through. Season with salt and pepper. Mix the dill with the mayonnaise and spread on both halves of the wholewheat roll. Arrange the cucumber and prawns on both halves and serve as an open sandwich garnished with the lime.

SERVES 1

Prawn & Mango Salad with Chilli Dressing

15 ml butter

15 ml olive oil

5 ml crushed garlic

24 large prawns, butterflied and deveined (leave the shell on)

100 g macadamia nuts (or cashews)

2 heads butter lettuce

1 head red oak lettuce

handful of rocket leaves

3 mangoes

juice of 3 limes

2 red chillies, seeded and chopped

10 ml crushed ginger

15 ml chopped fresh dill

5 ml fish sauce

5 ml sugar

salt and freshly ground black pepper

Melt the butter with the olive oil in a large saucepan over medium heat until it bubbles. Add the garlic and sauté the prawns for 2–3 minutes on each side, then set aside to cool. The prawns should be firm and rubbery and the flesh opaque – don't overcook them as they become powdery. Toast the macadamias in a dry pan over medium heat until they start to brown, then roughly chop them and set aside. Wash and drain the lettuce leaves and rocket and arrange on a large platter. Peel and slice the mangoes into slivers and arrange on the leaves with the prawns. Mix the lime juice with the chillies, ginger, dill, fish sauce and sugar, then season to taste. Scatter the macadamias over the salad and follow this with the dressing before serving.

SERVES 4–6

Smoked Salmon & Caviar Tart

23 cm tin lined with shortcrust pastry and baked blind (see Basics, page 216)

200 ml fresh cream

5 ml dill seeds

3 eggs

salt and freshly ground black pepper

200 g smoked salmon, julienned

60 g gruyère cheese, grated

about 60 ml caviar

Prepare the pastry shell beforehand. Preheat the oven to 180 °C (350 °F, Gas Mark 4). Whisk together the cream, dill seeds and eggs and season with salt and pepper. Arrange the smoked salmon and cheese on the base of the pastry shell. Pour the cream mixture over the salmon and bake for 20–25 minutes until the custard has just set. Serve each slice with a teaspoon of caviar on the top.

SERVES 4–6

Smoked Salmon Tagliatelle with Vodka

500 ml fish stock

375 ml fresh cream

zest and juice of 1 lemon

100 ml vodka

500 g smoked salmon

50 ml chopped fresh dill

salt and freshly ground black pepper

600 g fresh tagliatelle

olive oil

lemon wedges to garnish

In a large saucepan, bring the fish stock, cream, lemon zest and vodka to the boil. Reduce the heat and simmer to reduce until you are left with about 600 ml of thickened sauce. Julienne the smoked salmon and add with the dill, lemon juice, salt and pepper to the sauce, then remove from the heat immediately. Cook the tagliatelle in a large pot of salted water until *al dente*, then strain and drizzle with a little olive oil before tossing in the sauce and serving, garnished with lemon wedges.

SERVES 4–6

Prawn Curry

30 ml peanut oil	4 green chillies, seeded and finely chopped
1 large onion, finely chopped	
15 ml turmeric	1 x 410 g tin chopped tomatoes
5 ml ground coriander	1 x 410 g tin coconut milk
5 ml ground cumin	zest and juice of 1 lemon
2.5 ml chilli powder	150–200 ml water
1 stick cinnamon	5 ml sugar
3 cloves garlic, peeled and crushed	pinch of salt
1 thumb-sized piece root ginger, peeled and finely chopped	800 g medium prawns, deveined and shelled
5 ml grated nutmeg	1 bunch fresh coriander to garnish
20 curry leaves	

Heat the oil in a large saucepan and sauté the onion until soft and transparent. Add the turmeric, ground coriander, cumin, chilli powder, cinnamon, garlic, ginger, nutmeg, curry leaves and chillies and cook for 2–3 minutes. Stir in the chopped tomatoes, coconut milk, lemon zest and juice. Pour in the water and season to taste with sugar and salt. Bring to the boil, reduce the heat and leave to simmer on low for 10–15 minutes to allow all the flavours to infuse. Add the prawns and bring the curry back to the boil. Continue to cook for a further 8–12 minutes until the prawns are cooked through. Garnish with roughly torn coriander and serve with basmati rice, sliced banana and a cucumber salad.

SERVES 4

Russian Haddock Pie

1.5 kg haddock steaks

500 ml milk

400 g ready-to-roll puff pastry

FILLING

120 g butter

2 onions, finely chopped

120 g cake (plain) flour

1 litre milk

150 g grated Cheddar cheese

salt and freshly ground black pepper

60 ml chopped fresh parsley

juice of 2 lemons

Preheat the oven to 180 °C (350 °F, Gas Mark 4). Place the haddock in a roasting pan and pour over the 500 ml milk. Bake for 20–25 minutes until the fish starts to flake. Remove from the oven and set aside to cool.

Increase the oven temperature to 220 °C (425 °F, Gas Mark 7). Roll out the pastry just a little on a lightly floured surface and neaten the edges with a sharp knife. Transfer to a baking sheet and cook the whole rectangle for 15–20 minutes until well risen and golden. Slice the pastry horizontally through the centre and separate into two pieces the same size as the original rectangle. Bake for a further 5 minutes, then remove and leave to cool. Reduce the oven temperature to 180 °C.

To cook the filling, heat a large saucepan and melt the butter. Add the onions and sauté until soft. Add the flour and stir until well coated, then remove from the heat and pour in the milk, whisking constantly. Return to the heat and bring to the boil. The sauce must be thick. When thickened, stir in the cheese and season with salt and pepper. Flake the fish and add to the sauce with the chopped parsley and lemon juice. Stir gently. Place one half of the pastry onto a baking sheet and spoon the filling onto it. Cover with the other half and return to the oven at 180 °C for 15 minutes. Transfer to a serving platter and serve with the Avocado Salad with Dill & Yoghurt Dressing (page 21).

SERVES 6

Kingklip & Asparagus with Dill Hollandaise

2 bundles asparagus

4 kingklip fillets (they should be thick fillets of about 200–250 g each)

50 ml olive oil

sprigs of fresh dill to garnish

DILL HOLLANDAISE

250 g butter

1 lemon

6 egg yolks

salt and freshly ground black pepper

30 g chopped fresh dill

Make the hollandaise first by melting the butter gently in a saucepan until the milk solids separate. Juice the lemon and place the juice in a blender with the egg yolks. Blend until combined and, with the machine still running on a low speed, slowly pour in the hot butter, blending until pale yellow and thick. Season to taste and stir in the chopped dill.

To cook the asparagus, place in a large pot of salted water and bring to the boil. Snap off the last centimetre or two of the stalks and, when they are all done, place them in the boiling water for 3–4 minutes. Drain in a colander and refresh in cold water.

To cook the fish, preheat the oven to 180 °C (350 °F, Gas Mark 4). Heat a large skillet and fry the fish in the olive oil, skin side down, for 5 minutes. Turn and cook the other side for another 5 minutes. Transfer to a roasting dish and finish in the oven for 5–10 minutes until the fish just starts to flake. Arrange the asparagus on individual plates, top with the fish, garnish with dill sprigs and serve the sauce at the table.

SERVES 4

Pickled Fish

3 kg firm white fish fillets

salt and freshly ground black pepper

oil for frying

6 large onions, thinly sliced

1.5 litres white wine vinegar

500 ml water

5 ml turmeric

45 ml curry powder

2 red chillies

165 g apricot jam

150 g sultanas or raisins

Cut the fish fillets into individual portions and season with salt and pepper. Heat some oil in a large pan and fry the fish on both sides until golden brown. Remove from the pan and set aside. In the same pan, add a little more oil and fry the onions until soft, then set these aside with the fish. In a medium saucepan, heat all the other ingredients, except the sultanas or raisins, and bring to the boil. In a deep dish, layer the fish, onion rings and sultanas, then pour the hot liquid over the whole dish. Cover and leave to mature in the refrigerator for 2 days.

SERVES 8–10

Smoked Grunter

800 g coarse salt

3 litres water

3 medium grunter (or other suitable white fish), filleted

50 g oolong tea leaves

45 ml sugar

Mix the coarse salt and water together to form the brine for the fish. Place the fillets in the brine and leave to firm for 30 minutes. Remove the fillets from the brine and place on cooling racks over a roasting pan to dry for 1 hour. Prepare the smoker by forming three tin foil cups to place below the rack to smoke the fish. Place the oolong tea and sugar in these cups. Slowly heat the smoker on two plates (either electric or gas) over a medium heat. Once the smoker starts to produce some smoke, place the fish fillets skin side down on the rack. Cover and smoke for 45–60 minutes until the fillets are firm to the touch. Remove immediately from the heat and serve with the Green Bean Salad (page 22) or with fresh bread and horseradish cream.

SERVES 4–6

Breads & Savouries

We bake fresh bread every day on the farm. It's a staple and not easy to come by out in the sticks, but baking bread is also a wonderfully satisfying and therapeutic pastime. When we run our cooking courses, students learn a new bread recipe every day. We built a wood-fired outdoor oven in which to bake bread and one of our favourite things to do is to gather all the makings of a mezze platter and make focaccias to eat with them. In this chapter, our magpie obsession with collecting recipes is very evident and we have included recipes we brought back from Italy, Ireland, Mozambique and America.

Olive Bread

2.25 kg cake (plain) flour
20 ml salt
2 x 10 g packets instant yeast
750 ml warm water
15 ml olive oil
200 g pitted black olives, quartered

Mix the flour and the salt in a large bowl and sprinkle the yeast over the top. Add the warm water and mix with a wooden spoon until the dough is formed. Knead the dough either by hand or in a machine with a dough hook until the dough is smooth. Form into a smooth ball and rub all over with olive oil. Rub the inside of the bowl with some olive oil and place the dough in it. Cover with clingfilm and leave to rise until doubled in size. Line three colanders with lightly floured dishcloths, knock back the risen dough and divide into three equal portions. Flatten each portion and place a few quartered olives in the middle. Shape the dough back into a ball and place in a lined colander. Repeat this process until all the loaves are formed. Leave to rise again until doubled in size. Preheat the oven to 230 °C (450 °F, Gas Mark 8). When the dough has risen, invert it onto a lightly greased baking sheet and bake for 40–45 minutes until the bread sounds hollow when tapped underneath.

MAKES 3 LOAVES

Kitke Bread

1.2 kg cake (plain) flour
10 ml salt
5 ml sugar
40 g butter
1½ x 10 g packets (15 g) instant yeast
800–1 000 ml warm milk
1 egg yolk plus 10 ml milk
10 ml poppy seeds
10 ml sesame seeds (optional)

Place the flour, salt, sugar and butter in a large mixing bowl and rub all the ingredients together until the mixture resembles breadcrumbs. Sprinkle the yeast over the top, add at least 800 ml warm milk and knead the dough. If too dry, add a little more liquid at a time to form a soft dough. Knead well until smooth and the gluten has developed. Cover and leave to develop until doubled in size. Knock back and divide the dough into three equal portions. Roll into long, sausage-like shapes and plait together to form the traditional kitke shape.

Preheat the oven to 190 °C (375 °F, Gas Mark 5). Transfer the loaf to a greased baking sheet and brush with the egg yolk and milk mixture. Sprinkle with the seeds and bake in the oven for 45–60 minutes until firm and cooked. If it sounds hollow when tapped underneath, then the bread is properly cooked.

MAKES 1 LOAF

Portuguese Potato Bread

500 g mashed sweet potato* (cooked weight)
900 ml lukewarm water
1.5 kg cake (plain) flour
20 ml salt
1½ x 10 g packets (15 g) instant yeast

Preheat the oven to 220 °C (425 °F, Gas Mark 7) and grease two baking
sheets. Blend the sweet potato and warm water until smooth. Place all
the other ingredients in a separate bowl and make a well in the centre.
Add the blended sweet potato and knead into the dry ingredients. Turn
out onto a well-floured surface and knead until the dough is smooth
and elastic. Leave to rise in a warm place until doubled in size. Knock
the dough back and divide into four equal portions. Place two loaves on
each baking sheet. If making rolls, instead of dividing the dough into
four, pinch off pieces of roughly equal size, form into fat sausage shapes
and arrange on baking sheets. Be sure to leave enough room for the
rolls to rise during baking. Leave to rise again, then dust with flour.
Bake for 15 minutes, then reduce the oven temperature to 180 °C
(350 °F, Gas Mark 4) and bake the bread for 30–40 minutes and the
rolls for 10–15 minutes.

MAKES 4 LOAVES OR 24 ROLLS

* You can use regular potatoes too.

Sourdough Bread

Making sourdough bread is about practice and feel. This is not a recipe for first-time yeast users. This is our recipe and we have found that it works for us. It is important that you use fresh yeast and not dried or instant.

STARTER DOUGH
20 g fresh yeast
500 ml warm water
280 g cake (plain) flour

Place the yeast in a mixing bowl, add the water and stir until the yeast has dissolved. Add the flour and stir until well blended. Cover with clingfilm and leave to stand at room temperature for at least 48 hours. The starter will be bubbly, with a yellowish liquid on the surface. At this stage, remove 250 ml of the starter and set aside to make the bread. To the remaining starter add 140 g cake flour and 250 ml milk and blend well. Store in the fridge in a jar with a loose-fitting lid. Whenever using part of the starter it needs to be re-fed with 140 g cake flour and 250 ml milk as above.

BREAD

250 ml starter dough

10 g fresh yeast

500 g cake (plain) flour

5 ml salt

60 ml vegetable oil

5 ml sugar

375 ml lukewarm water

Place the starter dough and fresh yeast into a large bowl and mix
together until smooth. Add all the remaining ingredients and knead
in an electric mixer with a dough hook until the dough is as smooth as
a baby's bottom. Cover with clingfilm and leave to rise until doubled
in volume. Knock back and knead again on a lightly floured surface.
Divide into two equal portions and shape into loaves. Place on a
lightly greased baking sheet and leave to rise again while the oven
is preheated to 200 °C (400 °F, Gas Mark 6). Sprinkle the loaves with
some flour and bake for 20–25 minutes until golden brown and hollow-
sounding when tapped.

MAKES 2 LOAVES

Irish White Soda Bread

This bread is made from a recipe that Jason brought back from Darina Allen and her cooking school, Ballymaloe, in Ireland. We have it at least twice a week, preferably with fig jam.

500 g cake (plain) flour
5 ml salt
5 ml bicarbonate of soda
400 ml buttermilk or maas

Preheat the oven to 230 °C (450 °F, Gas Mark 8). Sift the dry ingredients and make a well in the centre. Pour in the liquid and, using one hand, mix in the flour from the sides of the bowl to form a ball. Turn out onto a floured surface and knead for a second to tidy it up. Place on a floured baking sheet and cut a cross in the top. Bake for 15 minutes, then reduce the oven temperature to 200 °C (400 °F, Gas Mark 6) and bake for a further 30 minutes until golden brown and hollow when tapped.

MAKES 1 LOAF

Potato Delights

2 potatoes, cooked and mashed through a ricer

420 g cake (plain) flour

60 g cold butter, grated

2.5 ml salt

30 ml baking powder

250 ml milk

Preheat the oven to 220 °C (425 °F, Gas Mark 7). Place the mashed potatoes, flour, grated butter, salt and baking powder in a bowl and add the milk. Knead together to form a dough. Roll out on a lightly floured surface and cut out rounds with a medium scone cutter. Place on a greased baking sheet and bake for 15–20 minutes until well risen and lightly browned. Serve hot with butter and a grape preserve or with home-made jam of your choice.

MAKES ABOUT 20

Focaccia

600 g cake (plain) flour

10 ml salt

5 ml sugar

1 x 10 g packet instant yeast

80 ml olive oil

up to 400 ml lukewarm water

3 cloves garlic, peeled and crushed

3 sprigs fresh rosemary

Maldon® sea salt and freshly ground black pepper

Place the flour, salt and sugar in a large bowl. Sprinkle the yeast over
the top and add 30 ml of the olive oil. Pour in half the water and bring
the flour mix and water together by hand. Add more water, a little at
a time, and knead together to form a soft but firm dough. Cover the
bowl with clingfilm and leave to prove in a draft-free place until
doubled in size.

Preheat the oven to 240 °C (475 °F, Gas Mark 9). Knock back the dough
and divide it into four or six equal portions. Mix the remaining olive oil,
garlic and rosemary in a small bowl. Roll out each piece of dough on a
lightly floured surface, then transfer to a large greased baking sheet.
Rub some of the herb oil all over the surface of the dough, then sprinkle
with sea salt and pepper. Bake for 20 minutes until the dough has
puffed up and is lightly browned and crispy.

MAKES 4–6

Aunty Nora's Bagels

750 g cake (plain) flour
500 ml lukewarm water
1 egg
½ egg shell (about 15 ml) sunflower oil
10 ml salt
1 x 10 g packet instant yeast
15 ml sugar
sesame seeds for sprinkling

Place all the ingredients, except the sesame seeds, in a large bowl and knead together until well combined and elastic. The dough must be stiffish – add more water if needed. Leave to rise until doubled in size.

Preheat the oven to 230 °C (450 °F, Gas Mark 8). Punch down the dough and divide and shape into 16 bagels. Leave to rise again on a floured dish towel. Bring a pot of water to the boil with 5 ml sugar and 5 ml salt. Add the bagels, two at a time, and boil for a count of 10 each time. Transfer to a greased baking sheet, sprinkle with sesame seeds and bake in the oven for 10 minutes until hollow sounding when tapped at the bottom.

MAKES 16

Mealie Bread (Cheat Version)

45 ml oil

250 ml milk

3 eggs

140 g cake (plain) flour

165 g mealie (maize) meal

15 ml baking powder

5 ml salt

100 g sugar

1 x 410 g tin creamed sweetcorn

Fill a large pot (it needs to be big enough to hold a 2-litre steamer) a quarter way with water and bring to the boil. Lightly grease a fluted steamer and set aside. In a bowl, beat the oil, milk and eggs together. Place all the dry ingredients in a separate bowl and pour the sweetcorn on top. Stir in the milk and egg mixture and combine well. Pour the batter into the prepared steamer and steam for 1½ hours. Serve inverted on a plate with home-made butter.

MAKES 1 LOAF

Mealie Bread

This is a very old, traditional recipe and is delicious with pickled fish, grilled chicken or guinea fowl, or pickled pork.

500 g fresh mealie kernels cut from the cob and minced
3 eggs
45 ml melted butter
50 g sugar
5 ml salt
125 ml sour cream
5 ml baking powder

Fill a large pot (it needs to be big enough to hold a 2-litre steamer) a quarter way with water and bring to the boil. Lightly grease a fluted steamer and set aside. Place all the ingredients in a large bowl and beat together until well combined. Pour into the steamer and place in the pot. Bring the water back to the boil, then reduce the heat to medium and leave the bread to steam for 2 hours. Remove from the heat and invert onto a serving plate. Best served with home-made farm butter.

MAKES 1 LOAF

Pissaladière

DOUGH

280 g cake (plain) flour

5 ml salt

½ x 10 g packet (5 g) instant yeast

300–400 ml warm water

10 ml olive oil

TOPPING

1 kg onions, sliced

45 ml olive oil

anchovy fillets and black olives to decorate (as many as you like)

salt and freshly ground black pepper

Make the dough by placing the flour, salt and yeast in a large bowl, add 300 ml water and the olive oil and knead together to form a coarse dough. Add more water if needed and knead the dough until smooth. Set aside to rise until doubled in size.

To prepare the topping, sauté the onions in the olive oil until soft and golden in colour, then set aside to cool. Knock back the risen dough and roll out on a lightly floured surface. Transfer to a large ovenproof pizza plate or tray. Place the sautéed onions on top and spread them evenly. Decorate with anchovies and olives and season with salt and pepper. Bake for 30–45 minutes in an outdoor oven or a conventional oven preheated to 240 °C (475 °F, Gas Mark 9). Serve with a green salad.

SERVES 6–8

Cheese Straws

100 g cake (plain) flour
90 g butter
100 g Cheddar cheese, grated
1 egg, beaten
caraway seeds for sprinkling
50 g Parmesan cheese, finely grated

Preheat the oven to 200 °C (400 °F, Gas Mark 6). In a food processor, blend the flour, butter and Cheddar cheese until it forms a ball. Wrap the dough in clingfilm and refrigerate for 20–30 minutes. Roll out on a lightly floured surface and brush the entire surface with beaten egg. Sprinkle with caraway seeds and Parmesan cheese and cut into fingers (1 cm x 10 cm). Bake for 10–15 minutes until lightly browned. Serve with a good red wine.

MAKES ABOUT 30

Fruit

It seems there's always some type of fruit ripening or blossoming on the trees at the farm. Over the 30 years we've lived here, we've planted a variety of fruit trees. There are plums, peaches, apricots, figs, crab apples, tree tomatoes, quinces and lemons. We also have a beautiful apple of a variety we've never been able to identify, courtesy of a foreign guest who dropped his apple core on that spot. Fruit just lends itself to making desserts, which we love preparing, and we are always looking for or testing recipes to preserve the stuff that the orchard produces. It's a great way to enjoy the taste of a particular fruit long after the season is over.

Apricot or Plum Jam

1 kg apricots or plums, stoned
750 g sugar

Place the stoned fruit in a large pot and cover with the sugar. Leave overnight to allow the fruit juices to be drawn out. Bring the mixture to the boil over a gentle heat, stirring constantly to ensure the sugar has dissolved before the mixture comes to the boil. Continue boiling over a high heat and stir occasionally so that the jam does not stick to the bottom of the pot. (It is important to boil at a high heat so that the jam sets quickly and does not overcook.) Check the setting consistency by either lifting the wooden spoon above the pot and allowing the mixture to drop from the spoon or leave a little of the mixture to cool on a saucer, then test the texture. This quantity of jam will take 15–20 minutes to cook.

Preheat the oven to 120 °C (250 °F, Gas Mark ½). While the jam is cooking, sterilize the bottles by placing them in the oven for 15 minutes. Remove and place on a tray, then spoon in the jam, leaving enough room below the rim to cover and seal with melted wax before closing tightly with a lid.

MAKES 4–5 HONEY JARS

Crab Apple Jelly

You need a large pot for this recipe.

6 kg crab apples, washed
water to cover
sugar

Halve the crab apples and place them in the pot. Cover with water to about 2 cm above the level of the fruit and bring to the boil. Reduce the heat and simmer gently for 2 hours, uncovered. Place a colander lined with a tea towel or muslin cloth over a second pot or large bowl. (Actually, you also need a big colander.) Remove the fruit from the heat and tip it into the colander. Leave the fruit to drain for 1 hour. Do not disturb it or press it in any way or you will get cloudy jelly. Discard the fruit – we feed it to the pigs – and measure the juice that you have strained off.

To make the jelly you will need 100 g sugar for every 250 ml juice. Place the juice and sugar together in a pot, bring to the boil, and then reduce to a simmer and allow it to cook away, uncovered, until the setting consistency is reached (if you dip a wooden spoon into it, drops should cling like thin honey rather than dripping off like water). Spoon the jelly into sterilized jars and seal with wax before closing the lids. It will keep for at least 6 months.

MAKES 6 MEDIUM BOTTLES

Tarte Tatin

This recipe comes with a cautionary note. As we tell all the students at our school, caramelized sugar is one of the most dangerous ingredients to work with in the kitchen. It has a high melting point and can cause a really nasty burn. Make sure you are focused on what you are doing – this is not a good recipe to prepare under pressure – and scoot the kids out of the kitchen.

10 Granny Smith apples (you may need more or less than 10 depending on their size)
125 g butter
250 g sugar
400 g ready-to-roll puff pastry

Preheat the oven to 230 °C (450 °F, Gas Mark 8). Peel, core and halve the apples and put them in water so they don't brown. In a 25 cm ovenproof pan, melt the butter and sugar together over medium heat, stirring constantly. It will bubble and foam a little at first, but it will settle and start to colour. As soon as it reaches a light caramel colour, remove it from the heat and carefully start to pack the drained apples, back to back, into the pan. Place in the oven for 15 minutes to cook the apples a little. Remove and allow to cool for 20 minutes.

Roll out the puff pastry and, using a sharp knife, cut a round 'lid' to fit the pan. Place the pastry on top of the pan, tucking it in around the edges. Prick holes with a fork or knife and bake for a further 30 minutes until the pastry is golden. Allow the tarte to cool slightly, hardening the caramelized sugar a bit before turning it out onto a plate.

SERVES 8

The Best Fig Jam

This is Colette's favourite jam and, as she says, it is like spreading summer on toast.

2 kg firm, ripe figs
5 ml fennel seeds
5 cm piece stick cinnamon
2 whole cloves
800 g sugar
500 ml water
zest of 1 lemon
60 ml lemon juice

Remove the stems and quarter the figs, then set aside. Make a little muslin bag to hold the fennel, cinnamon and cloves and tie it with string. Combine the sugar and water in a large pot and slowly bring to the boil. Remove from the heat and add the lemon zest, figs and the muslin bag. Stir and leave it to stand at room temperature for a few hours or overnight. Bring to the boil, then reduce the heat to medium and simmer until a thickened jam consistency is achieved. Add the lemon juice during the last 30 minutes of cooking. Discard the cloth bag and ladle the jam into sterilized jars.

MAKES 4 JAM JARS

Quince Preserve

10–12 ripe quinces, peeled and quartered

600 ml water

250 g sugar

2.5 ml grated nutmeg

Bring a medium pot of water to the boil. Place the prepared quinces in the boiling water and simmer for 15–20 minutes until just soft. In a separate saucepan, bring the 600 ml water and sugar to the boil, stirring constantly until all the sugar has dissolved. Add the softened quinces and nutmeg and bring to the boil once again. Remove from the heat and spoon the quinces into sterilized bottles. Make sure the fruit is covered with syrup, then seal while still hot. Serve with a cardamom cream or ice cream as a refreshing dessert.

MAKES 2 MEDIUM BOTTLES

Rhubarb & Banana Crumble

CRUMBLE

120 g cake (plain) flour

100 g butter

100 g sugar

50 g ground almonds

FILLING

12 sticks fresh rhubarb

3 ripe bananas

juice and zest of 1 lemon

120 g sugar

icing sugar for dusting

Preheat the oven to 180 °C (350 °F, Gas Mark 4) and butter 6 x 9 cm-diameter ramekins or ovenproof teacups. Place all the crumble ingredients in a food processor and blend until crumbly.

For the filling, roughly chop the rhubarb and slice the bananas and mix them together with the lemon juice, zest and sugar. Spoon this mixture into the ramekins and top with the crumble mixture. Bake for 20–25 minutes until golden brown. Unmould, dust with icing sugar and serve with fresh whipped cream or ginger ice cream.

SERVES 6

Rustic Nectarine Tart

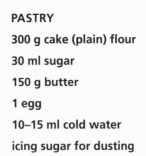

PASTRY

300 g cake (plain) flour

30 ml sugar

150 g butter

1 egg

10–15 ml cold water

icing sugar for dusting

FILLING

8 ripe nectarines, stoned and quartered

120 g sugar

juice of 1 lemon

15 ml cake (plain) flour

5 ml ground cinnamon

Make the pastry first by blending the flour, sugar and butter in a food processor until crumbly. Add the egg and some cold water to bind the pastry into a ball. Cover with clingfilm and leave to rest in the refrigerator for 30 minutes.

   In the meantime preheat the oven to 200 °C (400 °F, Gas Mark 6) and prepare the filling. Mix all the filling ingredients in a bowl. Roll out the pastry on a lightly floured surface and line a 20 cm pie dish so that the pastry overhangs quite a bit on the sides. Fill the pastry with the filling and fold the hanging pastry over the filling towards the middle, not covering the nectarine filling completely. Bake in the oven for 45–50 minutes. Remove from the pie dish, dust with icing sugar and serve with fresh whipped cream or custard.

SERVES 6–8

Citrus Pudding

Nigel Slater, one of our favourite food writers, inspired this recipe. We love his simple approach to cooking and flavour combinations.

125 g butter
180 g sugar
zest and juice of 1 lemon
zest and juice of 2 oranges
4 eggs, separated
70 g cake (plain) flour
500 ml milk

Preheat the oven to 180 °C (350 °F, Gas Mark 4). Grease a medium-sized heatproof mixing bowl with a little butter. Cream the butter, sugar and the zest of the lemon and oranges together until creamy white. Add the yolks to the butter mix and blend in well. Add the flour and milk alternately to get a smooth mixture. Stir in the orange and lemon juice. Beat the egg whites until stiff peaks form and fold into the mixture. Pour the mixture into the prepared bowl and cook in a *bain-marie* in the oven for 1 hour until the pudding is firm to the touch. Serve hot with pouring cream if desired.

SERVES 6

Fig Tarte Tatin

30 g butter
100 g sugar
3 cardamom pods, crushed
11 figs, halved
400 g ready-to-roll puff pastry

Preheat the oven to 230 °C (450 °F, Gas Mark 8). In a 25 cm ovenproof pan, melt the butter over medium heat. Add the sugar and crushed cardamom pods and allow to caramelize until lightly golden. Add the figs, cut side down, and cook over low heat for 5 minutes. Remove from the heat. On a lightly floured surface, roll out the puff pastry and cut out a 30 cm-diameter circle. Place this over the figs, pressing the pastry down gently. Prick holes in the pastry with a fork or knife. Bake in the oven for 30–35 minutes until the pastry is golden brown and cooked. Allow to cool for 10 minutes before inverting onto a serving platter. Serve with fresh whipped cream.

SERVES 8

Roasted Figs

Figs go very well with poultry and are particularly good with game birds.

10–12 fresh figs
10–12 fresh bay leaves
60 ml melted butter
salt and freshly ground black pepper

Preheat the oven to 220 °C (425 °F, Gas Mark 7). Place the figs in a roasting dish and cut a slit down the middle of each one. Place a bay leaf in the slit and pour the butter over evenly. Season with salt and pepper and roast in the oven for 20–25 minutes until the figs are soft and slightly browned. Serve with roast chicken.

As a dessert variation of this recipe, omit the bay leaves, salt and pepper, and drizzle with honey before roasting. Serve with mascarpone or ice cream.

SERVES 6

Orange Soufflé Crêpes

The crêpes have to be filled at the last minute and placed under the grill and then sauced. Make sure you've prepped everything ahead of time.

CRÊPES	ORANGE SAUCE
140 g cake (plain) flour	375 ml orange juice
3 eggs	50 ml sugar
250 ml milk	125 ml Van der Hum liqueur
125 ml water	15 ml cornflour mixed with
15 ml oil	a little water
15 ml brandy	
icing sugar for dusting	FILLING
	2 egg whites
CHOCOLATE SAUCE	1 x crème pâtissière recipe
150 g dark chocolate	(page 220)
250 ml fresh cream	

Prepare the crêpes first. Beat all the ingredients together, except the icing sugar, until smooth. Place in the refrigerator and leave to rest for 30 minutes. Heat a non-stick crêpe pan and fry a little mixture at a time. Flip over and cook the other side. Set aside until ready to serve.

To make the chocolate sauce, melt the chocolate and cream together in a double boiler and stir until smooth. Serve at room temperature.

To make the orange sauce, bring all the ingredients to the boil for 5 minutes. Serve hot.

To make the filling, beat the egg whites until stiff, then fold them into the crème pâtissière.

To assemble, fill the crêpes and fold into a triangular shape. Place each filled crêpe on a serving plate and grill until the custard mixture puffs up and is slightly browned. Pour both sauces over and dust with icing sugar.

MAKES ABOUT 10

Steamed Date & Banana Pudding

Sukey, my mother's stepmother, couldn't boil an egg when she married my grandfather. However, she turned out to be an excellent cook and this is one of our favourite Sukey recipes.

BATTER	LEMON SAUCE
125 g butter	250 ml water
100 g sugar	100 g sugar
2 eggs	15 ml cornflour
75 g chopped dates	45 g butter
2 ripe bananas, mashed	lemon juice and grated nutmeg
140 g cake (plain) flour	to taste
5 ml baking powder	
2.5 ml bicarbonate of soda	
pinch of salt	
125 ml milk	

To make the batter, cream the butter and sugar together in a food processor. Add the eggs, one at a time, and blend until creamy. Add the dates, bananas, dry ingredients and milk and blend well. Spoon the batter into a lightly greased 2-litre steamer and cover securely with a lid. Steam for 2 hours, then invert onto a plate.

To make the lemon sauce, whisk the water, sugar and cornflour together in a small saucepan and bring to the boil, whisking constantly to prevent any lumps forming. Remove from the heat and add the butter, lemon juice and nutmeg. Serve the pudding hot, with the hot sauce passed separately.

SERVES 8–10

Preserved Tree Tomatoes (Tomatillos)

200 g sugar
375 ml water
10 tomatillos, peeled and halved

Place the sugar and water in a saucepan and bring to the boil, stirring
constantly until all the sugar has dissolved. Add the tomatillos and bring
the mixture back to the boil. Simmer for 7–10 minutes until the fruit is
soft. Spoon into a sterilized bottle, making sure the fruit is tightly
packed and covered with liquid, then seal tightly. Serve with fresh
yoghurt for breakfast.

MAKES 1 LARGE BOTTLE

Stewed Guavas

400 g sugar
500 ml water
10 firm, ripe guavas, peeled and halved

Bring the sugar and water to the boil in a large saucepan, stirring constantly until all the sugar has dissolved. Add the guavas and simmer for 10 minutes until the fruit is cooked. Transfer into sterilized, warm bottles, making sure the fruit is covered in syrup. Seal and store in the refrigerator for no longer than 4 weeks. The guavas can be eaten as soon as they're cold.

MAKES 1 LARGE BOTTLE

Peach Chutney

2 kg peaches, stoned (do not peel)

2 medium Granny Smith apples, peeled

2 thumb-sized pieces ginger, peeled and crushed

4 cloves garlic, peeled and crushed

2 medium onions, quartered

1 x 410 g tin chopped tomatoes

600 ml white wine vinegar

600 g sugar

30 ml Maldon® sea salt

10 ml ground cinnamon

15 ml grated nutmeg

15 ml ground white pepper

Place the peaches, apples, ginger, garlic and onions in a food processor and blend until fine. Transfer to a large pot and add the remaining ingredients. Bring to the boil, then reduce the heat to medium and leave the chutney to cook for at least 1 hour until thick and gooey. Stir occasionally to prevent sticking. Spoon into sterilized bottles and seal while still hot.

MAKES 4–6 MEDIUM BOTTLES

Lemon Cordial

This is a fantastic, refreshing drink and is a wonderful way to use surplus lemons. Mint can be added to a jugful to add zing.

500 ml lemon juice
400 g sugar

Stir the lemon juice and sugar together until the sugar has dissolved. Pour the liquid into a sterilized bottle and refrigerate. Before serving, dilute with ice and soda.

MAKES 1 LITRE

Clementine Vodka

1 kg clementines
500 g sugar
2 sticks cinnamon
8 cardamom pods, crushed
1.5 litres vodka

Juice the clementines and place the juice in a large bowl with half the squeezed fruit. Add the remaining ingredients and stir until the sugar has dissolved. Decant into sterilized bottles and seal. Store in the refrigerator for 8 weeks before consumption, shaking the bottle once a week to make sure all the ingredients are combined. The vodka will keep for 6 months.

MAKES ABOUT 3 LITRES

Elderberry Elixir

This recipe is inspired by Antonio Carluccio. It is great for soothing cold symptoms, especially an irritating cough.

2.5 kg elderberries, washed and picked
250 ml water
7 cardamom pods
15 whole cloves
2 sticks cinnamon
juice and zest of 2 lemons
1.2 kg sugar
600 ml whisky, brandy or dark rum

Place the berries and the water in a saucepan and boil for 20 minutes until all the berries have burst. Squash the berries against the side of the pan to release all the juice. Leave to cool, then strain through a muslin-lined colander and squeeze out all the juice. (You can also use a tea towel for this and squeeze it out by hand.) Place the resulting liquid in a pot with all the spices, lemon juice and zest. Bring to the boil and cook for 10 minutes, then add the sugar and stir until all the sugar has dissolved. Cook for a further 10 minutes and add the alcohol of your choice. Pour into sterilized bottles, seal and store in the refrigerator for at least 1 month before using. This will keep in the fridge for at least 6 months.

MAKES ABOUT 1.5 LITRES

Cakes & Treats

There are a couple of recipes that we are constantly asked for by people visiting the farm. They tend to be of the sweet variety, in the form of cakes or other treats, and everyone has their particular favourite. Camilla loves to bake and we have the best basic ingredients available to us in the form of fresh farm eggs and butter. Wherever possible, we also try to source organic flour to enhance the whole experience, and if no one is asking for his or her favourite, we just make whatever we fancy on any given day.

Carrot Cake

250 g grated carrot

1 x 440 g tin pineapple rings, drained

150 g chopped pecan nuts

4 eggs

300 g sugar

200 ml oil

280 g cake (plain) flour

10 ml baking powder

7 ml bicarbonate of soda

5 ml salt

15 ml ground cinnamon

CHANTILLY CREAM (OPTIONAL)

250 ml fresh cream

30 ml sugar

5 ml vanilla essence

lavender flowers to decorate

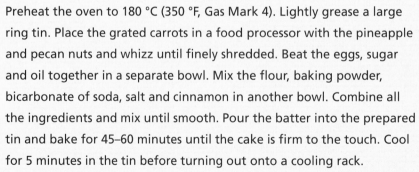

Preheat the oven to 180 °C (350 °F, Gas Mark 4). Lightly grease a large ring tin. Place the grated carrots in a food processor with the pineapple and pecan nuts and whizz until finely shredded. Beat the eggs, sugar and oil together in a separate bowl. Mix the flour, baking powder, bicarbonate of soda, salt and cinnamon in another bowl. Combine all the ingredients and mix until smooth. Pour the batter into the prepared tin and bake for 45–60 minutes until the cake is firm to the touch. Cool for 5 minutes in the tin before turning out onto a cooling rack.

To make the topping, beat the cream, sugar and vanilla until stiff. Spread over the cooled cake and decorate with lavender flowers.

SERVES 10–12

Sukey's Christmas Fruitcake

This is a steamed Christmas cake and can be made two months in advance. Store wrapped in tin foil in an airtight tin.

500 g butter	125 ml good brandy
500 g sugar	30 ml golden syrup
8 eggs	5 ml vanilla essence
720 g cake (plain) flour	5 ml lemon essence
2.5 ml salt	5 ml almond essence
5 ml mixed spice	5 ml bicarbonate of soda
2 kg fruit cake mix (with candied peel)	250 g glacé cherries

Line two cake tins with greaseproof paper and make a double-layered cover of greaseproof paper to form a lid for each tin. In an electric mixer, cream the butter and sugar very well. Beat in the eggs, one at a time, beating well after each addition. Add all the remaining ingredients, except the cherries, and mix until well blended. Divide the mixture between the tins. Arrange the cherries on top of both cakes and push them halfway in. Smooth over the top with a spatula, cover each tin with its cover and secure tightly with string. Steam in a large pot with some water for 3 hours over a low heat. Add more water if necessary during the cooking process. Once done remove the cake, take off the cover and bake in a preheated oven at 160 °C (325 °F, Gas Mark 3) for 45–60 minutes until the cake is nicely browned. Brush the top with another 125 ml brandy and cool in the tin. Invert and peel away the paper lining. Wrap and store.

MAKES 2 x 20 CM-DIAMETER, DEEP CAKE TINS (NOT LOOSE BOTTOM)

Cupcakes

125 g butter

125 g sugar

2 eggs

60 ml milk

10 ml vanilla essence

125 g self-raising flour

ICING

125 g butter

195 g icing sugar

5 ml vanilla essence

30–45 ml milk

To make the cupcakes, preheat the oven to 180 °C (350 °F, Gas Mark 4) and line a muffin tray with paper cookie cups. Cream the butter and sugar together and add the eggs, one at a time. Beat in the milk and vanilla essence. Add the flour and blend until smooth. Divide the mixture evenly between the 12 paper cups and bake for 20–25 minutes until well risen and firm to the touch. Allow to cool before decorating.

To make the icing, cream the butter until soft. Add the icing sugar and vanilla essence and beat together with enough milk until soft and fluffy. Divide the icing into little bowls and colour with food colouring. Ice the cupcakes and decorate as desired.

MAKES 12

192

Almond Cake

250 g soft butter

300 g castor sugar

6 eggs

200 g ground almonds

90 g cake (plain) flour

50 ml Kirsch or Amaretto liqueur

icing or castor sugar for dusting

Preheat the oven to 180 °C (350 °F, Gas Mark 4) and lightly grease a
20 cm loose bottom tin. Cream the butter and sugar together in a food
processor until light and fluffy. Add the eggs, one at a time, beating
well after each addition. Add the almonds. Fold in the flour and liqueur,
then spoon the batter into the prepared tin. Bake for 1 hour, then allow
to cool in the tin. Remove the cake from the tin and place on a cake
stand. Dust with icing or castor sugar and serve. This cake matures well.

SERVES 8

Ginger Nuts

250 g butter

450 g cake (plain) flour

450 g sugar

15 ml mixed spice*

20 ml ground ginger

5 ml ground cinnamon

2 eggs

15 ml milk

30 ml golden syrup

10 ml bicarbonate of soda

Preheat the oven to 140 °C (275 °F, Gas Mark 1) and lightly grease three baking sheets. In a large bowl, rub the butter into the flour, then add the sugar and spices. In a separate bowl, whisk the eggs, milk, golden syrup and bicarbonate of soda together. Add the wet ingredients to the dry ingredients and knead until well combined. Roll the mixture into balls the size of walnuts and place on the prepared baking sheets. Press each ball down with your thumb and bake for 40 minutes until crisp and golden. Cool on a wire rack.

MAKES 50–60 BISCUITS

* Add an extra 5 ml mixed spice and omit the ground ginger to change the flavour of the biscuits.

The Farm Apple Cake

For this recipe you can substitute the same quantity fresh pears for apples. This is very simple to make and keeps for 2–3 days if it isn't all devoured straight from the oven.

1 kg Granny Smith apples
225 g sugar
60 ml milk
2 eggs
170 g cake (plain) flour
pinch of salt
60 g flaked almonds
5 ml ground cloves
5 ml baking powder
60 g butter

Preheat the oven to 190 °C (375 °F, Gas Mark 5). Grease a 20 cm cake tin and coat with flour. Peel and core the apples and place in a bowl of water. Beat the sugar, milk and eggs until pale in colour. Add the flour, salt, half the almonds and the cloves and beat to combine. Add the baking powder to the cake mixture. Slice the apples and stir them into the batter. Spoon the batter into the cake tin. Dot the top with butter and sprinkle with the remaining almonds. Bake for 50 minutes until golden brown. Serve with double thick cream.

SERVES 8

Norenius Bun

Granny Sukey's very good Scandinavian friend, Mrs Norenius, gave her this gorgeous recipe for a quick and easy tea cake.

PASTRY	FILLING
280 g cake (plain) flour	75 g soft butter
pinch of salt	65 g sugar
60 g butter	10 ml ground cinnamon
15 ml sugar	150 g dried fruitcake mix
15 ml baking powder	
1 egg	ICING
60 ml milk	130 g icing sugar
	2.5 ml almond essence
	water to thin
	glacé cherries to decorate (optional)

Preheat the oven to 200 °C (400 °F, Gas Mark 6). To make the pastry, place the flour, salt, butter, sugar and baking powder in a food processor and blend until the mixture is crumbly. Add the egg and milk and blend to form a ball. On a lightly floured surface, roll out the pastry to form a 30 x 20 cm rectangle.

For the filling, spread the pastry with the softened butter and sprinkle with sugar, cinnamon and cake mix. Roll up to form a long sausage and seal the ends. Bend into a C-shape and place on a greased baking sheet. Bake for 20–25 minutes, then remove from the oven and cool for about 10 minutes. Mix the icing sugar, almond essence and enough water to make a soft icing and ice the warm bun. Decorate with cherries if desired.

SERVES 6–8

Chocolate Ice Cream

400 g good quality dark chocolate

250 ml boiling water

50 ml sugar

5 eggs, separated

1 litre fresh cream

½ x 397 g tin condensed milk

Place the chocolate, boiling water and sugar in a blender and blend until smooth. Add the egg yolks, one at a time, and blend together. Set aside. In a large mixing bowl, beat the cream until soft peaks form. Add the condensed milk, then the chocolate mixture. Whisk the egg whites until stiff and fold into the chocolate mixture. Pour into a 2 litre ice-cream container and freeze overnight.

MAKES 2 LITRES

Ginger Ice Cream

1 thumb-sized piece root ginger, peeled and thinly sliced

300 ml fresh cream

300 ml milk

6 egg yolks

150 g sugar

5 pieces preserved ginger, finely chopped

Just cover the ginger slices with water and bring to the boil over high heat. Simmer for 2 minutes, then drain. In a saucepan, place the cooked ginger, cream and milk and bring to a gentle simmer. Remove from the heat and leave to infuse for 1–2 hours. In a bowl, beat the egg yolks and sugar together until pale and thick. Pour in the milk and ginger mixture and mix together. Transfer the mixture to the top of a double boiler and cook, stirring continuously, until the mixture is thick and coats the back of a metal spoon. Take care not to let it boil. Strain through a sieve and add the preserved ginger. Refrigerate to cool completely, then freeze the cooled mixture in an ice-cream maker according to the manufacturer's instructions.

MAKES ABOUT 1 LITRE

Oeufs à la Neige

MERINGUE

8 egg whites

300 g sugar

**100 g chopped nuts or 100 g desiccated coconut mixed with
 sugar as a topping**

CRÈME ANGLAISE

750 ml milk

1 vanilla pod

8 egg yolks

45 ml sugar

To make the meringue, preheat the oven to 160 °C (325 °F, Gas Mark 3) and grease 8 x 9 cm-diameter ramekins. Prepare the chosen topping before starting. Whisk the egg whites until soft peaks form, then add the sugar in a steady stream, whisking continuously. Spoon the meringue into ramekins and pile high. Sprinkle on the topping and bake in a *bain-marie* for 20–30 minutes.

   To make the crème anglaise, scald the milk with the vanilla pod, remove from heat and leave to infuse for 10 minutes. In the meantime, beat the egg yolks with the sugar. Pour the milk into the yolks and strain into a double boiler. Cook, stirring continuously, until the custard coats the back of a spoon. Divide the custard between eight serving bowls. Turn the meringues out of the ramekins and float them in the custard.

SERVES 8

Strawberry Choux Pastries

CHOUX PASTRY

125 g butter

250 ml boiling water

140 g cake (plain) flour

4 large (51–61 g) eggs

FILLING

250 ml fresh cream

1 quantity crème pâtissière (page 220)

50 ml Van der Hum liqueur

12–15 large ripe strawberries

icing sugar for dusting

To make the pastry, preheat the oven to 200 °C (400 °F, Gas Mark 6). In a small saucepan, add the butter to the boiling water and heat until the butter has melted. Add the flour all at once and stir vigorously with a wooden spoon until the mixture forms a ball. Remove from the heat and cool for exactly 5 minutes (set a timer). Add the eggs, one at a time, beating well after each addition. The mixture should still hold its shape. Pipe swirls of the mixture onto a lightly greased baking sheet. Bake for 25 minutes, then prick each pastry with a knife to release the steam. Return to the oven for 5 minutes. Remove and leave to cool completely.

   To make the filling, whip the cream until stiff and fold it into the cooled crème pâtissière together with the liqueur. Hull and slice the strawberries so that they are small enough to fit through an unfluted piping nozzle. Fold the strawberries into the cream mixture and place in a piping bag with a large nozzle attached. Slice the pastries, then pipe the filling into each one to fill. Dust liberally with icing sugar and serve.

SERVES 6–8

Hot Chocolate

1 red chilli, seeded

50 g sugar

1 stick cinnamon

1.5 litres milk

75 g cocoa powder

50 g dark chocolate, roughly chopped

Place the chilli, sugar, cinnamon and milk in a saucepan and bring to the boil. Remove from the heat and leave to infuse for 10 minutes. Discard the chilli and cinnamon stick and whisk in the cocoa powder and chocolate. Return to the heat and cook until the mixture boils, whisking constantly. Add sugar to taste. Serve in mugs.

SERVES 4–6

Basics

Our experience in running the cooking school has taught us a great deal about cooking, particularly about perfecting the basics of recipes. If you can get the basics right and produce a beautiful stock or authentic pasta, you are more than halfway towards preparing a memorable meal. A good hollandaise can turn steamed asparagus into a feast. Sometimes we do these things so often at the farm that it becomes like second nature and we forget how easy it is to teach these skills. This section is about the basics that you may need to produce the recipes in this book – take the time to practise, test and get them right because this knowledge and preparation is the basis of being a good cook.

Chicken Stock

2–3 raw chicken carcasses, chopped	6 peppercorns
3.75 litres water	1 sprig fresh thyme
1 onion, sliced	5 parsley stalks (remove the leaves so as not to
1 stick celery	colour the stock)
1 carrot, sliced	1 bay leaf

Place all the ingredients in a stockpot and bring to the boil. Skim the fat off the top with a tablespoon. Reduce the heat to low and continue to simmer for 3–5 hours. Remove from the heat, strain and leave to cool completely in the refrigerator overnight so that you can peel away any congealed fat before use. The stock can keep for 3 days in the refrigerator or can be decanted into containers and frozen until needed. **MAKES ABOUT 2.5 LITRES**

Beef Stock

1 kg beef marrow bones	2 sticks celery, chopped
1 onion, halved	1 bouquet garni (selection of fresh herbs tied
3 carrots, chopped	together with string)

Preheat the oven to 230 °C (450 °F, Gas Mark 8). Place the marrow bones, onion, carrots and celery in a large roasting pan and roast for 20–25 minutes until all the ingredients are well browned. This step is very important, as it will ensure a coloured stock. Transfer the browned ingredients to a large stockpot and fill with water to just cover, then add the bouquet garni. Bring to the boil, then reduce the heat and simmer for 3 hours, removing the scum off the top if necessary. Strain the stock. Keeps for 3 days in the refrigerator and is perfect for freezing. **MAKES 2 LITRES**

Game Stock

2 kg game bones
2 carrots, chopped
2 sticks celery, chopped
1 bay leaf
6 peppercorns
250 ml dry white wine

Preheat the oven to 230 °C (450 °F, Gas Mark 8). Place the bones in a roasting pan and roast for 20–25 minutes until well browned. Transfer to a stockpot with the remaining ingredients and cover with water. Bring to the boil, then reduce heat and leave to simmer for 3 hours until you have a rich stock. Strain. Keeps for 3 days in the refrigerator and is perfect for freezing. **MAKES 3 LITRES**

Red Wine Sauce

500 ml home-made beef stock (page 210)
500 ml dry red wine
1 clove garlic, peeled and crushed
roux (equal parts butter and flour) to thicken
salt and freshly ground black pepper

Place the stock, wine and garlic in a saucepan and bring to the boil. Reduce the heat and simmer until the liquid has reduced by half. Thicken with the roux until the sauce has the thickness of pouring cream. Season to taste. **MAKES ABOUT 500 ML**

Butter

The amount of butter produced by 2 litres of cream can vary remarkably depending on the fat content of the cream.

2 litres fresh cream   **non-iodated salt**

Pour the cream into the bowl of a mixer. Fit the whisk utensil and start off by beating fast. You have to monitor this process and reduce the speed as the butter starts to form and separates from the buttermilk. As it starts to get thick, you need to fit a K-beater or the whisk will be damaged. The butter will become a large, hard mass. Drain off the buttermilk. You can either discard this or use it for baking. Rinse the butter under cold running water. When the water runs clear, it is ready. Add salt to taste and mix it in well, then pat into shape and wrap in greaseproof paper or spoon into containers.

Baked Polenta

1 litre water and/or milk	**3 eggs**
5 ml salt	**50 g Parmesan cheese, grated**
200 g coarsely ground yellow maize meal	**freshly ground black pepper and grated nutmeg**
45 g butter	**to taste**

Preheat the oven to 160 °C (325 °F, Gas Mark 3). Bring the water to the boil or scald the milk, then add the salt and maize meal and whisk until smooth. Bring to the boil, whisking continuously to ensure there are no lumps. Reduce the heat and allow to simmer for 15 minutes, stirring occasionally, until the mixture has thickened. Remove from heat and whisk in the butter, eggs and cheese. Season with black pepper and nutmeg. Pour into an ovenproof container and bake for 45 minutes until the dish is set and the crust is golden brown. **SERVES 8**

Parsley Couscous

250 ml water	45 g butter
5 ml salt	freshly ground black pepper
250 g quick-cooking couscous	30 ml chopped fresh parsley

Place the water in a saucepan with the salt and bring to the boil. Remove from the heat and stir in the couscous with a wooden spoon. Set aside for 2 minutes to allow it to swell. Return to the heat and stir in the butter with a fork, breaking up any lumps as you go. Season with salt and pepper and add the parsley just before serving. **SERVES 4**

Red Wine Onion Marmalade

3 medium onions, sliced	200 g sugar
10 ml olive oil	500 ml red wine

Place the onion slices in a large bowl of water for 30 minutes. Heat the olive oil in a large saucepan, drain the onions and fry until translucent. Add the sugar and red wine and bring to the boil. Reduce the heat to medium and allow to reduce until almost all the wine has evaporated and the onions are a dark cabernet red colour. **MAKES 1 JAM JAR**

Nasturtium Vinegar

40 nasturtium flowers, washed	1 litre white wine vinegar

Push the nasturtium flowers through the top of a clean vinegar bottle. Pour in the vinegar. Seal with a lid and leave to infuse for 3 days. Use in salad dressings. **MAKES 1 LITRE**

Hollandaise

250 g butter	4 egg yolks
1 lemon	salt and freshly ground black pepper

Melt the butter gently in a saucepan until the milk solids separate. Juice the lemon and place the juice in a blender with the egg yolks. Whizz this mixture until combined then, with the machine still running on a low speed, slowly pour in the hot butter. Blend until pale yellow and thick. Season to taste. For a variation that's excellent with fish, stir in 100 g chopped fresh dill. **MAKES 300 ML**

Mayonnaise

1 egg (room temperature)	250 ml sunflower oil
juice of 1 small lemon (room temperature)	salt and freshly ground black pepper

Place the egg and lemon juice in a blender and blend together for 1 minute. With the blender still running on low speed, pour in the oil in a slow, constant stream until the mixture emulsifies and thickens. Season to taste. Transfer the thick mayonnaise to a serving bowl. **MAKES 300 ML**

Chilli Aïoli

3 cloves garlic, peeled	juice of 1 small lemon
1 red chilli, seeded and chopped	250 ml sunflower oil
1 egg	salt and freshly ground black pepper

Place the garlic, chilli, egg and lemon juice (all at room temperature) in a blender and blend for 1 minute. With the blender still running on low speed, pour in the oil in a gentle stream until the mixture emulsifies. Season to taste. Transfer to a serving bowl and serve with beef fillet. **MAKES 300 ML**

Mashed Potatoes

1 kg potatoes, peeled and quartered	250 ml milk
50 g butter	salt and freshly ground black pepper
15 ml extra virgin olive oil	4 ml grated nutmeg

Place the potatoes in a large pot of boiling salted water. Continue to boil until cooked. Drain and push the soft potatoes through a potato ricer* into a bowl. Add the butter and olive oil and mix together with the milk. Do this with a whisk to remove any lumps. Season with salt, pepper and nutmeg. **SERVES 4–6**

* You can also use a potato masher, but a ricer makes better, fluffier mash with no lumps.

Artichoke Mash

1 kg potatoes, peeled and quartered	50 g butter
350 g Jerusalem artichokes, scrubbed	salt and freshly ground black pepper
juice of ½ lemon	6 spring onions, chopped
200 ml fresh cream	

Place the potatoes in a large pot of salted water. Bring to the boil, reduce the heat and simmer for 45–50 minutes until cooked. Place the scrubbed artichokes and lemon juice in a medium-sized pot and cover with salted water. Bring to the boil, then reduce the heat and simmer until soft – about 30–40 minutes. Drain both the potatoes and artichokes and mash through a ricer or use a potato masher. Add the cream and butter and blend by hand until smooth. Season with salt and pepper. Sprinkle the spring onions on top and serve with oxtail. **SERVES 6–8**

Yorkshire Puddings

280 g cake (plain) flour   4 eggs

pinch of salt   100 ml sunflower oil

500 ml milk

Place the flour and salt in a bowl. Beat the milk and eggs together. Beat the milk mixture into the flour until smooth, then transfer into a jug and refrigerate for at least 3 hours until well chilled.

Preheat the oven to 230 °C (450 °F, Gas Mark 8). Pour 5 ml sunflower oil into each section of a muffin tray and heat in the oven for 3 minutes until hot. Three-quarter fill each section with chilled Yorkshire pudding mixture and bake for 15 minutes. Reduce the oven temperature to 200 °C (400 °F, Gas Mark 6) and bake for a further 15–20 minutes until well risen and golden brown. Serve with French roast fillet and red wine sauce. **MAKES 18**

Shortcrust Tart Pastry

150 g butter   1 egg

280 g cake (plain) flour   cold water to bind

Place the butter and flour in a food processor and blend until crumbly. Lightly beat the egg and add while the food processor is still running. Add a little cold water if the mixture is too dry. Blend until a ball forms. Cover the pastry in clingfilm and chill for 30 minutes.

Line a 23 cm tart tin or a rectangular tart pan with the pastry. Cover with a sheet of greaseproof paper, fill with dried beans and bake blind in a preheated oven at 200 °C (400 °F, Gas Mark 6) for 15–20 minutes. Remove the beans and bake for a further 5 minutes to ensure that the bottom is cooked. **MAKES ENOUGH TO LINE A 23 CM TART TIN**

Bottled Tomatoes

The recipe below is for a litre jar of tomatoes, but it would be easier to do several jars at a time. Simply double the recipe as many times as the tomatoes you have available and can fit in a pot at one time.

1 kg ripe tomatoes

Slice an X at the base of each tomato and place in a large bowl. Pour enough boiling water over them to cover and leave to stand for about 5 minutes. Remove the skins and cut out any unsavoury bits. Pack closely into a 1-litre jar and seal tightly. Place a rack at the bottom of a large pot and half fill the pot with water. Place the jars on the rack, put the lid on the pot and bring to the boil. Steam the jars in the covered pot for about 30 minutes. The circulating steam will cook the tomatoes in their own juices.

Tomato Concassée

2 x 400 g tins whole peeled tomatoes   **60 ml olive oil**
4 cloves garlic, peeled and crushed   **salt and freshly ground black pepper**
15 ml sugar

Place the tomatoes in a food processor and blend until well chopped (don't overdo it or you'll end up with tomato purée). Place in a pot with the garlic, sugar, olive oil and salt and pepper to taste. Cook over medium heat, uncovered, until the mixture has thickened – about 45 minutes. This can be served on fresh tagliatelle with Parmesan cheese and basil. You can use your own bottled tomatoes for this recipe too. **MAKES 600 ML**

Fresh Pasta

300 g cake (plain) flour   3 eggs

Place the flour in a food processor fitted with the dough hook. Add the eggs and blend together to form a ball. If the dough is too dry, add a little water and if too wet add a little more flour. Remove from the food processor and knead further with your hands until smooth. Cover with an inverted bowl for 30 minutes before rolling. The secret to making good pasta is to knead the pasta very well to develop the gluten and to allow the dough to rest for at least 30 minutes before rolling.

Divide the dough into 8–10 walnut-sized portions. Set up the pasta machine and, starting with the lowest setting (no. 1), start rolling the dough through the machine. Refold the dough and go through this setting 2–3 times, then through the no. 2 setting 2–3 times. Keep dusting with flour so the dough doesn't stick. Go through all the settings and cut the strips in half if they become too long to handle. Allow the strips to dry for 3–4 minutes before cutting into desired shapes. Once cut, the pasta can be hung up to dry and then stored until needed.

To cook the pasta, bring a large pot of water to the boil with 45–60 ml coarse salt. Add the pasta and cook until *al dente*. For fresh wet pasta this will take 4–5 minutes; dry pasta will take a little longer. Serve with a sauce of your choice. **SERVES 8**

Ginger Beer

This is a cold-water ginger beer recipe and must be stored in the refrigerator. It can be made in the early morning and will be ready to drink by lunchtime. The ginger beer should be used within 4–5 days.

8 litres water   10 g brewer's yeast
800 g sugar   3 x 20 ml bottles Jamaica ginger

Mix all the ingredients briskly. Make sure that all the sugar dissolves. Pour into bottles and cork. Store in the refrigerator and serve chilled. **MAKES 8–9 LITRES**

Chocolate Sauce

35 g icing sugar   60 ml golden syrup

25 g cocoa powder   60 ml water

60 g butter

Place all the ingredients in a saucepan and bring to the boil. Serve with ice cream. **MAKES 250 ML**

Crumpets

350 g cake (plain) flour   375 ml milk

10 ml baking powder   2 eggs

pinch of salt   30 ml melted butter

Place the flour, baking powder and salt in a medium-sized bowl. In a separate bowl, whisk the milk, eggs and melted butter together. Stir the wet ingredients into the dry ingredients to form a smooth batter. Heat a pan over medium heat and add a tablespoonful of the mixture. Cook until the crumpet bubbles on the top, then flip over and cook the other side. Remove from the pan and keep warm in a kitchen towel until all the mixture is cooked. Serve warm with butter and honey or golden syrup.
MAKES ABOUT 24

Ice-cream Cones

200 g butter	375 g cake (plain) flour
250 g sugar	250 ml water
4 eggs	

In a food processor, cream the butter and sugar together until creamy. Add the eggs, one at a time, and blend well after each addition. Add the flour and water and process until smooth. Spoon a table-spoonful of the mixture onto a heated cone iron, close the lid and cook until golden brown. Remove and curl into a cone shape over the handle of a wooden spoon while still hot. They cool rapidly, so work quickly, using gloves if you find them too hot to handle. Serve with your favourite ice cream. **MAKES 16 CONES**

Crème Pâtissière

250 ml milk	30 g cake (plain) flour
2 eggs yolks	30 g butter
60 g vanilla-infused sugar	a little sugar for sprinkling

In a small saucepan, scald the milk then remove from heat. In a small bowl, beat together the egg yolks and sugar until thick. Add the flour and continue to beat until smooth. Gently pour in the heated milk, whisking constantly, then strain back into the saucepan and return to the heat. Cook over a gentle heat, whisking constantly, until the mixture has thickened and just come to the boil. Remove and add the butter. Sprinkle a little sugar on the surface to prevent the custard from forming a skin. Cover with clingfilm and set aside to cool. **MAKES ABOUT 400 ML**

Conversion Charts

METRIC	US CUPS	IMPERIAL
2.5 ml	½ tsp	–
4 ml	¾ tsp	–
5 ml	1 tsp	3/16 fl oz
15 ml	1 Tbsp	½ fl oz
60 ml	4 Tbsp (¼ cup)	2 fl oz
80 ml	⅓ cup	2¾ fl oz
125 ml	½ cup	4½ fl oz
160 ml	⅔ cup	5½ fl oz
200 ml	¾ cup	7 fl oz
250 ml	1 cup	9 fl oz
100 g	–	3½ oz
250 g	–	9 oz
500 g	–	1 lb
750 g	–	1¾ lb
1 kg	–	2¼ lb

OVEN TEMPERATURES

CELSIUS (°C)	FAHRENHEIT (°F)	GAS MARK
100 °C	200 °F	¼
110 °C	225 °F	¼
120 °C	250 °F	½
140 °C	275 °F	1
150 °C	300 °F	2
160 °C	325 °F	3
180 °C	350 °F	4
190 °C	375 °F	5
200 °C	400 °F	6
220 °C	425 °F	7
230 °C	450 °F	8
240 °C	475 °F	9

250 ML (1 CUP)/WEIGHT COMPARISON

Cake (plain) flour	140 g
Sugar	200 g
Maize (mealie) meal	165 g
Cornflour	120 g
Grated cheese (Cheddar, Gouda)	100 g
Desiccated coconut	80 g
Dried fruit (cake mix, raisins)	150 g
Whole nuts	100 g
Chopped nuts	150 g

Recipe Index

Page numbers in **bold** indicate photographs.